Quasi-Judicial Proceedings
(Under the Indian Legal Framework)

I0474018

Quasi-Judicial Proceedings
(Under the Indian Legal Framework)

CHIDAMBARAM RAMESH

www.createspace.com

Copyright:	© **Chidambaram Ramesh**
Published by:	Createspace.com
Printed from:	United States of America
First Published:	July 2012

ISBN-13:978-1478203162

ISBN-10: 1478203161

Disclaimer

While every effort has been made to avoid any mistake or omission, this publication is being sold on the condition and understanding that neither the author nor the publishers would be liable in any manner to any person by reason of any mistake or omission in this publication or for any action taken or omitted to be taken on advice rendered or accepted on the basis of this work. The information contained in the book is for general application only. It does not offer legal advice for any specific cases and specific legal questions should be referred to an advocate/counsel. The content is the personal opinion of the author and does not necessarily represent the views or practices of the organization he belongs to.

*To my Grandmother Meenakshi Murugesu who
instilled in me the values of hard work*

Indian Law Journal Abbreviations used in the book

AIR: All India Reporter
BomLJ: Bombay Law Journal
BomLR: Bombay Law Reporter
CalLJ: Calcutta Law Journal
CeyLJ: Ceylon Law Journal
CLJ: Cambridge Law Journal
CLR: Current Law Reports
FJR: Factories Journal Reports
FLR: Factories and Labour Reports
ILR: Indian Law Reports
Ker LT: Kerala Law Times
Lab IC: Labour and Industrial Cases
LLJ: Labour Law Journal
LLN: Labour Law News
LLR: Labour Law Reporter
MLJ: Madras Law Journal
SCC: Supreme Court Cases
SCC(Supp): Supreme Court cases (Supplementary)
SCR: Supreme Court Reports
SLJ: Services Law Journal
SLR: Services Law Reporter

The administration of justice is the firmest pillar of government

- George Washington

INDEX

CHAPTER 8
Powers of the Inquiry Officer under the Code of Civil Procedure, 1908

Order V: Issue and Service of Summons

Order IX: Appearance of Parties and Consequence of Non-Appearance

CHAPTER 9
Relevant Provisions of the Indian Penal Code, 1860
Section 193 of IPC: Punishment for False Evidence, Giving or Fabricating False Evidence – Meaning of:
Section 196 of IPC: Using Evidence Known to be False
Section 228 of IPC: Intentional Insult or Interruption to Public Servant sitting in Judicial Proceeding
Civil Prison: Detention and Release

CHAPTER 10
Conclusion

APPENDIX-
    Important Judicial Pronouncements relating to quasi-judicial proceedings
    List of Important Legal Terms

Bibliography

Preface

Mark Twain humorously put it, '*Good judgment is the result of experience, and experience the result of bad judgment.*' This applies more to administrative adjudicators than to conventional judges. Officers appointed to hold quasi-judicial functions must have judicial approach and also knowledge and expertise in the constitutional, administrative and other related laws. The Supreme Court in the case of *K.Jain vs. Union of India and Ors* [(1993) 4 SCC] underlined the importance of legal training to quasi-judicial officers who preside over the Tribunal instituted under Articles 323-A and 323-B of the Constitution. It observed, 'It is necessary that those who adjudicate upon these matters should have legal expertise, judicial experience and modicum of legal training as on many an occasion, different and complex questions of law which baffle the minds of even trained judges in the High Court and Supreme Court would arise for discussion and decision.' Traditionally, the task of a quasi-judicial functionary was thought to be mechanical – a matter of applying rules and norms and less complex. Today, their functions are so complex that they cannot be expected to learn everything as they go along. More often than not, persons occupying the quasi-judicial chair are administrative and technical heads who do not have academic training in judicial sphere..

A properly developed departmental training module may ensure the actions of the officers conducting quasi-judicial functions are uniform and consistent with the rules and instructions. In the absence of such pre-conditioning, poor decisions are often made until judgement improves through extensive experience of the individual. Improving one's judgemental prowess through mistakes and failures is certainly not the optimal way. The decisions they take concerns, on the one hand, the rights of the citizens and on the other the interests of the State.

This book is an attempt, within the compass of a small volume, to help officers who often occupy quasi-judicial chair understand the elements of a quasi-judicial proceeding, ingredients of procedural due process and in reaching decisions that are so fair and equitable as to withstand the judicial scrutiny by Courts of law. The book also gives the Inquiry Officers a better understanding of what factors the Courts will consider and appreciate when their orders are appealed against.

I hope that this book contributes to the knowledge on the subject of quasi-judicial proceedings and it stands as a pioneering effort into a neglected but significant part of the process of quasi-judicial decisions. Over the years, a great many people have assisted me with the thinking and research that culminated in this book. I am thankful to every one of them.

Chidambaram Ramesh

Vellore

CHAPTER 1
INTRODUCTION

WHAT IS QUASI-JUDICIAL?

The epithet *'Quasi-judicial'* is popular in administrative parlance. Etymologically, it consists of two Latin words: *Quam* + *Si*. *Quam*, in Latin, means 'as much as' and *Si* means 'if.' The prefix *'quasi'* connotes the meaning – 'similar to but not exactly the same as.' As a prefix, the term 'quasi' found places in literature since 18th century and most productively in the 20th century[1]. It refers to those actions and powers exercised by the administrative agencies that are required to investigate or ascertain the facts and draw conclusions, in which there are hearings, orders, judgments or other activities similar to those conducted by judiciary. Thus, quasi-judicial proceedings are *similar to but not exactly court proceedings*. The term also implies that these authorities are not routinely responsible for holding such proceedings and often may have other duties also. In short, an administrative function is called 'quasi-judicial' when there is an obligation to assume the judicial approach and to comply with the basic requirements of natural justice. Thus, the fundamental purpose of a quasi-judicial hearing is to provide the affected parties *due process*. Due process requires notice of the proceedings and an opportunity to be heard.

Normally, the quasi-judicial body can make a decision that then becomes legally binding, unless appealed against. At the point where an appeal takes place, the case often moves into another quasi-judicial authority of higher order or into the traditional judicial system. The judge, in such cases, may not be in the role of assessing the facts of the case in particular, but rather simply be charged with determining whether the quasi-judicial entity made a decision it had the authority to make, and was within the confines of the law and any administrative rules and particularly whether

---

[1] http://www.etymonline.com

the principles of natural justice and doctrine of fairness have been complied with.

ADMINISTRATIVE VIS-À-VIS QUASI-JUDICIAL DECISIONS

The difference between an administrative decision and a quasi-judicial decision is blurred more often than not. Granting of a licence to a school is an administrative action while cancellation or suspension of it falls under the quasi-judicial domain. Why is it so? The decisions flowing out of a quasi-judicial function is likely (not always) to adversely affect upon the person – a matter of conflicting interest between an affected/aggrieved person and the interests of the State. When the administrative decisions are arrived at *subjectively*, according to the circumstances and on cost-benefit analysis of various factors, quasi-judicial decisions are *'objective'* – that is, based on facts and material evidences placed before the inquiring authority during the course of hearing. Here, one should note the difference between *'objective'* and *'subjective'* decisions. *Objective decisions* are those completely unbiased, verifiable by facts or performing mathematical calculations. *Subjective decisions*, on the other hand, are coloured by the individual personality of the decision-maker and often reality-based. It cannot be verified by using facts and figures. It may vary according from person to person. In other words, the difference between a subjective and an objective decision is the difference between *a fact* and *an opinion*. For instance, a statement that 'the table is having four legs' is an objective statement. It can be verified by anyone and the answer will be the same. A statement like 'the table is of good quality' is a subjective statement. It can hardly be verified with facts and figures nor would everyone agree with the statement. The degree of quality will differ from observer to observer according to the individual opinion. Quasi-judicial orders are fact-based and therefore objective decisions. Though administrative orders need not disclose the reasons[2] thereof, quasi-

---

[2] In India, the Law Commission in its 14th Report relating to judicial administration has recommended that in the case of administrative decisions also, reasons should be spelt out so that the judiciary can test the validity of the decisions easily.

judicial decisions ought to spell out its reasons. A purely administrative act does not decide any rights of private parties though it may affect them. But a quasi-judicial act determines private rights with a binding force[3]. An administrative act may be non-statutory and does not necessarily require statutory authority. But a body is called quasi-judicial only when it has statutory authority to discharge the function in question. A purely administrative body has no procedural obligation, unless it is specifically imposed by state[4]. But as soon as function is held to be 'quasi-judicial', the law requires that the rules of natural justice must be observed in discharging that function[5]. While an administrative or ministerial function may be delegated, a judicial or quasi-judicial function cannot, in the absence of express statutory provision, be delegated[6]. What distinguished a judicial from an administrative decision is that the decision of a Court is objective, i.e., arrived at by the application of fixed standards; even the discretion which a Court of Justice is allowed to exercise in some particular cases, has to be exercised in accordance with certain fixed principles[7]. On the other hand, the decisions of administrative authorities are usually subjective in the sense that they are reached without applying any standard at all, except that of expediency or policy[8].

Finally, as laid down by Justice Hedge, in the *A.K.Kraipak vs Union of India*[9], the dividing line between an administrative

---

[3] [*R. v. Dublin Corpn.*, (1878)2 Ir. 371(367) : *R. v. Local Govt. Bd.*, (1902)2 I.R. 349(373).]
[4] [*E.G. Frankin v. Minister of Town & Country Planning*, reported in (1947)2 All E.R. 289(295) H.L. ; *University of Celyon v. Fernande*, reported in (1960)1 All E.R. 631(637) P.C. ; *Ridge v. Baldwin*, reported in (1963)2 All E.R. 66(75; 86; 109].
[5] [*Union of India v. Verma*,]
[6] [*Vine v. National Dock Labour Bd.*, reported in (1959)3 All E.R. 393(950) H.L].
[7] [Sharp v. Wakefield, reported in (1891) A.C. 173(179)]
[8] [*Labour Relations Board v. J.E.I. Works*, reported in (1949) A.C. 134(149)] (*G.J. Kanga And Anr. v S.S. Basha* on 18 August, 1992, 1982).
[9] (1969) 2 SC 262: AIR 1970 SC 150.

19

power and the quasi-judicial power is quite thin and is gradually being obliterated. What was considered as an administrative power some years back is now being considered as a quasi-judicial power.

GROWTH OF QUASI-JUDICIAL INSTITUTIONS

Quasi-judicial institutions have a hoary past. The scheme to entrust certain specific issues to tribunals to decide on was initially an *ad hoc* measure. Tribunals (literally the word '*tribunal*' means '*seat of justice*') were set up to deal with specialized nature of issues which warranted technical expertise. Later, with the rise and growth of welfare state in the beginning of the last century, tribunals were preferred to ordinary courts due to their inexpensiveness, easy accessibility and expeditiousness in disposal of cases. After the World War II, large scale introduction of social welfare legislations such as Provident Fund Act, Insurance Act, Unemployment benefit etc., warranted institution of specialized bodies to handle disputes over such matters. The ordinary courts of law had already been overburdened with the pending volume of litigations. These factors facilitated the extension of discretionary powers to the executive arms of the State to adjudicate matters falling within their respective domains.

In India, the passing of the 42nd Constitutional Amendment in 1976 paved the way for institution of tribunals as a part of Indian justice delivery system. By this amendment, Article 323-A for constitution of the Administrative Tribunal and Article 323-B for constitution of other Tribunals for matters like Taxation, Foreign Exchange, Industrial and labour issues, Land reforms etc., were introduced and incorporated in the Constitution. The fact that the provisions relating the Central Administrative and other tribunals are provided separately under Part XIV-A of the Constitution and not under Part V and VI (which exclusively deal with judiciary) connotes the point that the tribunals are not supposed to function exactly as a court.

In pursuance of the power conferred upon it by clause (1) of article 323-A of the Constitution, Parliament enacted the Administrative Tribunals Act, 1985 (Central Act 13 of 1985). The Statement of Objects and Reasons of the Act indicates that it was in the express terms of article 323A of the Constitution and was being enacted because a large number of cases relating to service matters were pending before various courts; it was expected that 'the setting up of such Administrative Tribunals to deal exclusively with service matters would go a long way in not only reducing the burden of the various courts and thereby giving them more time to deal with other cases expeditiously but would also provide to the persons covered by the Administrative Tribunals speedy relief in respect of their grievances'. Pursuant to the provisions of the Act, the Central Administrative Tribunal, with five Benches, was established on November 1, 1985. Today, there are 17 Benches of the Tribunal located throughout the country wherever the seat of a High Court is located, with 33 Division Benches. In addition, circuit sittings are held at Nagpur, Goa, Aurangabad, Jammu, Shimla, Indore, Gwalior, Bilaspur, Ranchi, Pondicherry[now, Puducherry], Gangtok, Port Blair, Shillong, Agartala, Kohima, Imphal, Itanagar, Aizwal and Nainital. Apart from the Central Administrative Tribunal, there are also various tribunals set up by the government to take care of specific kinds of cases. Income Tax Appellate Tribunal, Intellectual Property Appellate Tribunal, Railway Claims Tribunal, Appellate Tribunal for Electricity, Debts Recovery Tribunal, Central Excise Service Tax Appellate Tribunal, EPF Appellate Tribunal are to name a few.

Thus with the growth of the governments and increasing nature of complexities of issues has come the phenomenal growth of quasi-judicial tribunals, boards and commissions in the administrative branches all over the world and India is no exception.

CHAPTER 2
PRINCIPLES OF NATURAL JUSTICE

We have seen the quasi-judicial proceedings are required to comply with the principles of natural justice. This raises the question, what is meant by '*natural justice*'? It is in fact difficult to define precisely what is meant by natural justice and it has to be understood in the context of various case laws. In the case of *Swadeshi Cotton Mills vs Union of India*, the Supreme Court of India held that the phrase 'natural justice' is not capable of a static and precise definition. It cannot be imprisoned in a strait-jacket of a cast-iron formula; it has kaleidoscopic view which varies according to fact situations.

Justice Krishna Iyer succinctly puts it, 'natural justice is a pervasive facet of secular law where a spiritual touch enlivens legislation, administration and adjudication, to make fairness a creed of life, it has many colours and shades, many forms and shapes and, save where valid law excludes, it applies when people are affected by acts of authority. It is the bone of healthy government, recognized from earliest times and not a mystic testament of judge-made law.'

The aim of the rules of natural justice is to secure justice, or, to put it negatively, to prevent miscarriage of justice[10]. In India, the judiciary has been consistently insisting on the observance of the principles of natural justice. The Law Commission of India has also recommended that the tribunals performing quasi-judicial functions should conform to the principles of natural justice and should act with openness, fairness and impartiality[11]. It recommended even a separate enactment laying down a simple procedure embodying the principles of natural justice that all quasi-judicial forums can follow them uniformly. Though the term 'natural justice' is difficult to define precisely, the basic postulates of its principle are easy to enumerate.

---

[10] [*A.K.Kraipak v. Union of India*, (1969) 2 SC 262: AIR 1970 SC 150].
[11] Law Commission of India 14th Report, 1958, page 695

BASIC POSTULATES OF PRINCIPLE OF NATURAL JUSTICE

Natural justice essentially encompasses three elements:

- No one shall be a judge in his own cause [*Nemo judex in causa sua*]

- No man shall be condemned unheard [*Audi alteram partem*]

- Justice should not only be done but should manifestly and undoubtedly be seen to be done[12].

No One Shall Be a Judge in His Own Cause

It means that the quasi-judicial authority must be impartial and act in good faith. He should adjudicate the matter before him with a detached and dispassionate mind. A person with a foreclosed mind or a person who has prejudged the issue or predetermined to punish the delinquent should not act as inquiry officer. The principle does not confine to a case where the Judge is an actual party but to cases where he has remote interest also. Similarly a person who is a complainant, or witness or prosecutor cannot act as a judge.

No Man Shall Be Condemned Unheard

'*Audi alteram partem* means each party must have the chance to present his version of the facts and to make submissions relevant to his case. It requires that a party should have the opportunity of adducing all relevant evidence on which he relies, that the evidence of the opponent should be taken in his presence, and that he should be given the opportunity of cross-examining the witness examined by that party, and that no material should be relied on against him without his being given an opportunity of explaining them' [*Union of India v. T.R.Verma*][13]. In the above case, the Supreme Court laid down the following three conditions,

---

[12] Lord Hewart put it in his famous judgement in 1923
[13] (1958) S.C.R.499, 507 ('57) A.SC.882

the compliance of which amounts to compliance of the dictums of principles of natural justice.

(i)   The adjudicator should receive all the relevant material which a party wishes to submit in his support.

(ii) The evidence of the opponent, whether oral or documentary, should be taken in his presence.

(iii) Each party should have the opportunity of rebutting the evidence of the other by cross-examination and explanation.

If hearing is not given by the adjudicating authority to the person concerned and the principles of natural justice are violated, the order is void and it cannot be justified on the ground that hearing *'would make no difference'* or *'no useful purpose would have been served'*.

Thus, in *Board of High School vs Kumari Chitra[14]*, the Board cancelled the examination of the petitioner [who had actually appeared at the examination] on the ground that there was shortage in attendance at lectures. But no notice was given to her before proceeding with the action. When the action was challenged, it was contended by the Board that the facts were not in dispute and hence 'no useful purpose would have been served' by giving a Show Cause notice to the petitioner. The Supreme Court set aside the decision of the Board, holding that the Board was acting in a quasi-judicial capacity and therefore it must observe the principles of natural justice.

When the parties fail to make use of the opportunities afforded to them viz., being absent without assigning reasons, or filing no reply to the notices, then there will be no violation of the principles of natural justice. Likewise, the authority conducting quasi-judicial proceedings is under no obligation to adjourn the hearings *suo moto* unless prayed for by the parties.

---

[14] (1970) 1 SCC 121 : AIR 1970 SC 1039.

In *Delhi Transport Corporation* vs*D.T.C. Mazdoor Congress and Others*[15] Ray, J. opined, 'It is now well settled that the *"audi alteram partem"* rule which in essence, enforces the equality clause in Article 14 of the Constitution is applicable not only to quasi-judicial orders but to administrative orders affecting prejudicially the party-in-question unless the application of the rule has been expressly excluded by the Act or Regulation or Rule...Rules of natural justice do not supplant but supplement the Rules and Regulations. Moreover, the Rule of Law which permeates our Constitution demands that it has to be observed both substantially and procedurally.'

Justice Should Not Only Be Done But Should Manifestly And Undoubtedly Be Seen To Be Done

It is now settled law that every judicial order must be supported by reasons. The justification underlying this judicial insistence is well illuminated by the Supreme Court of India's observations in *'Siemens Engineering vs Union of India and Another'*[16]:

When an authority makes an order in exercise of a quasi-judicial function, it must record its reasons in support of the order it makes. Every quasi-judicial order must be supported by reasons.

'If courts of law were to be replaced by administrative authorities and tribunals and with the proliferation of administrative law, they may have to be so replaced, it is essential that administrative authorities and tribunals should accord fair and proper hearing to the persons sought to be affected by their orders and give sufficiently clear and explicit reasons in support of the orders made by them. The rule requiring reasons to be given in support of an order is like the principle of *audi alteram partem*, a basic principle of natural justice which must inform every quasi-judicial process and this rule must be observed in its proper spirit and mere pretence of compliance with it would not satisfy the requirement of law.'

---

[15] 1991 Supp (1) SCC 600
[16] 1976 AIR 1785, 1976 SCR 489

SUBSIDIARY PRINCIPLES OF NATURAL JUSTICE

BIAS NEED NOT BE PROVED – REASONABLE DOUBT OR SUSPICION OF BIAS IS SUFFICIENT

A person who is thought to gain directly or indirectly any advantages from a decision is excluded from acting on behalf of authority. For this purpose, an actual exercise of bias need not be proved with unmistakable clarity, if the facts grew grounds for reasonable apprehension of a mere likelihood of bias, even if there is no real bias.

The principle has been laid down over and over again that persons who are exercising judicial functions must be in an entirely impartial position. They ought not to have any interest, pecuniary or otherwise, in the subject-matter of the litigation, and they must not be in such a position that any bias in favour of one side or the other can be imputed to them. Actual bias need not be proved, if the relationship is such that bias may seem likely [*P.D. Shamdasani vs The Central Bank Of India Limited*][17].

The law is as stated by De Smith's *Constitutional and Administrative Law*, New Edition at pages 584-85 :

If an adjudicator is likely to be biased he is also disqualified from acting. Likelihood of bias may arise from a number of causes; membership of an organization of authority that is a party to the proceedings; partisanship expressed in extra-judicial pronouncements; the fact of appearing as a witness for a party to the proceedings; personal animosity or friendship towards a party; family relationship with a party; professional or commercial relationships with a party; and so on. The categories of situations potentially giving rise to a likelihood of bias are not closed [*M. Koteswara Rao vs Apsrtc, Tirupati And Ors*][18].

ONE WHO DECIDES MUST ALSO HEAR

This principle is corollary of the judicial requirement of 'application of mind'. He who hears the case can apply his mind.

---

[17] (1938) 40 BOMLR 904
[18] 1997 (3) ALD 491, 1997 (3) ALT 68, (1997) IILLJ 489 AP

One person hearing the case and another deciding the matter results in 'divided responsibility' and 'non-application of mind' which vitiates the principles of natural justice. In the case of *Gullapalli Nageshwara Rao vs A.P.State Transport Corporation*[19] a scheme for nationalization of bus routes was notified by the state government. Objections raised by the petitioners against the government's scheme were heard by the Secretary to the Government, Department of Transport. But the material facts and other records were placed before the Chief Minister (who was also the Minister for Transport) for decision. Striking down the decision, the Supreme Court observed,

'Personal hearing enables the authority concerned to watch the demeanour of the witnesses and clear up his doubts during the course of the arguments, and the party appearing to persuade the authority by reasoned argument to accept his point of view. If one person hears and another decides, then personal hearing becomes an empty formality. We therefore hold that the said procedure followed in the case also offends another basic principle of judicial procedure.'

But this principle does not get affected in cases where one officer gives a hearing and receives evidences and on his transfer, promotion, or death, another officer hears the matter again after affording opportunities to the parties concerned, appreciates the material facts on record afresh and comes to conclusion.

ORAL HEARING IS SUFFICIENT

It is pertinent that the defendant should be offered sufficient opportunities to make his submissions – both oral and written. However, if he is allowed to submit written representations only and is not afforded a chance of oral hearing, it alone will not make the hearing illegal. In the case of *Union of India vsJ.P.Mitter*[20], the Supreme Court refused to quash the order of the President of India, in respect of a dispute regarding the age of a High Court Judge. It was held that where a written representation is allowed, and if the adjudicating authority is of the

---

[19] AIR 1959 SC 308
[20] 1971 AIR 1093, 1971 SCR (3) 483

opinion that the disputed question may be decided without giving the defendant an opportunity of personal hearing, there is no violation of natural justice.

In *M.P.Industries vs. Union of India*[21], Justice Subba Rao observed, 'it is no doubt a principle of natural justice that a quasi-judicial tribunal cannot make any decision adverse to a party without giving him an effective opportunity of meeting any relevant allegations against him. But the said opportunity need not necessarily be by personal hearing. It can be by written representation. Whether the said opportunity should be by written representation or by personal hearing depends upon the facts of each case and ordinarily it is in the discretion of the tribunal.'

The House of Lords has given a clear steer on the common law in R.(West) vsParole Board; (R)Smith v Parole Board (No.2)(2005) UKHL 1 [2005], 1 W.L.R 350. The procedure must be fair. The right to an oral hearing depends upon an assessment of a variety of factors: What is the nature of the issue? What are the circumstances? What is the legal and administrative context? What does the public interest require? Are the facts in issue? Are the facts likely to be in issue?

EX-POST FACTO HEARING

Ex-post facto hearing may be afforded in exceptional cases. The omission to serve the summons/notice on the defendant may also be considered under the category of exceptional cases and ex-post facto hearing may be offered to the defendants.

The decision of the Apex Court in *Maneka Gandhi* illustrates the application of the principle of *ex-post facto* hearing. In this context, the Court observed that in certain situations an action may be taken without affording prior hearing. However, as soon as action is taken, hearing should be given to the affected party so that the party may present his case and controvert that of opposite party.

---

[21] AIR 1966 SC 675.

It may however be noted that ex-post facto hearing is always inferior to hearing before decision and should be used on extremely exceptional circumstances to avoid strictures of Courts.

The Hon'ble Supreme Court of India, in the case of *Swadeshi Cotton Mills vs Union Of India*[22], quoted the words of Prof. De Smith, the renowned author of 'Judicial Review'.

'Can the absence of a hearing before a decision is made be adequately compensated for by a hearing *ex-post facto*? A prior hearing may be better than a subsequent hearing, but a subsequent hearing is better than no hearing at all; and in some cases the courts have held that statutory provision for an administrative appeal or even full judicial review on the merits are sufficient to negative the existence of any implied duty to hear before the original decision is made. The approach may be acceptable where the original decision does not cause serious detriment to the person affected, or where there is also a paramount need for prompt action, or where it is impracticable to afford antecedent hearings.'

The Apex Court in *Canara Bank and Others vsSri Debasis Das and others*[23] has discussed in detail the ingredients of natural justice and '*audi alteram partem*.' The observations made in the said judgment could be summarized as follows:

- Natural justice is another name of commonsense justice.

- Rules of natural justice are not codified canons. But they are principles ingrained into the conscience of man.

- Natural justice is the administration of justice in a commonsense liberal way.

- Justice is based substantially on natural ideals and human values.

- The administration of justice is to be freed from the narrow and restricted considerations which are usually

---

[22] 1981 AIR 818, 1981 SCR (2) 533
[23] AIR 2003 Supreme Court 2041

29

associated with a formulated law involving linguistic technicalities and grammatical niceties.

- It is the substance of justice which has to determine its form.

- The expressions 'natural justice' and 'legal justice' do not represent a watertight classification. It is the substance of justice which is to be secured by both and whenever legal justice fails to achieve this solemn purpose, natural justice is called in aid of legal justice.

- Natural justice relieves legal justice from unnecessary technicality, grammatical pedantry or logical prevarication. It supplies the omissions of a formulated law.

- As Lord Buckmaster said, 'no form or procedure should ever be permitted to exclude the presentation of a litigants' defence.'

- The adherence to principles of Natural Justice as recognized by all civilized States is of supreme importance when a quasi-judicial body embarks on determining disputes between the parties, or any administrative action involving civil consequences is in issue.

- Notice is the first limb of the principle of *Audi Alteram Partem*. Notice should apprise the party the case he has to meet. Adequate time should be given to make his representation.

Thus, the principle of natural justice cannot be restricted to the two maxims – '*audi alteram partem*' and '*nemo judex in causa propria*.' They include as well the right of the defendant to know on what criteria and after what reasoning the administrative authority came to its decision.

PRINCIPLES OF NATURAL JUSTICE NOT FOLLOWED – IMPLICATIONS OF

Article 14, 19, 21 of the Constitution lay down the cornerstone of natural justice in India. In the case of *E P Royappa vs. State of Tamilnadu*[24], the apex court held that a properly expressed and authenticated order can be challenged on the ground that condition precedent to the making of order has not been fulfilled or the principles of natural justice have not been observed. In another landmark case of *Maneka Gandhi vs. Union of India*[25], the apex court held that law which allows any administrative authority to take a decision affecting the rights of the people, without assigning the reason for such action, cannot be accepted as a procedure, which is just, fair and reasonable, hence violative of Articles 14 and 21 of the Consitution.

The Supreme Court of Nigeria, in the case of *Adedeji vsPolice Service Commission*[26] decreed as follows.

We are therefore not satisfied that when the circumstances of this case are looked into, adequate opportunity was given to the appellant to meet the case or the facts of the case known to the Commission. It is possible that the appellant is corrupt and did commit the offence alleged against him, that is not what we have to consider. Was the case against him sufficiently brought home to him that one can say that the requirements of natural justice were sufficiently observed on the facts and circumstances? ... We hereby order that the writ should go and the letter dismissing the appellant is hereby declared inoperative, void and of no effect.

In the famous *Maneka Gandhi vs Union of India*[27], the Apex Court discussed the increasing importance of Natural Justice and observed that Natural Justice is a great humanizing principle intended to invest law with fairness and to secure justice and over the years it has grown in to a widely pervasive rule. The Supreme

---

[24] AIR, 1974 SC 555
[25] (1978) 1 SCC 248: AIR 1978 SC 597
[26] (1968) NMLR 102
[27] [AIR 1978 Supreme Court 1978]

Court extracted a speech of Lord Morris in the House of Lords which is very interesting.

'That the conception of natural justice should at all stages guide those who discharge judicial functions is not merely an acceptable but is an essential part of the philosophy of the law. We often speak of the rules of natural justice. But there is nothing rigid or mechanical about them. What they comprehend has been analysed and described in many authorities. But any analysis must bring into relief rather their spirit and their inspiration than any precision of definition nor precision as to application. We do not search for prescriptions which will lay down exactly what must in various divergent situations, be done. The principle and procedures are to be applied which, in any particular situation or set of circumstances, are right and just and fair. Natural justice, it has been said, is only "fair play in action." Thus, the soul of natural justice is fair play in action and that is why it has received the widest recognition throughout the democratic world. In the United States, the right to an administrative hearing is regarded as essential requirement of fundamental fairness. And in England too, it has been held that "fair play in action" demands that before any prejudicial or adverse action is taken against a person, he must be given an opportunity to be heard. The rule was stated by Lord Denning, M.R. in these terms in Schmidt v. Secretary of State for Home Affairs: - 1962)2 Ch.D 149 "Where a public officer has power to deprive a person of his liberty or his property, the general principle is that it has not to be done without his being given an opportunity of being heard and of making representations on his own behalf."

UNNATURAL EXPANSION OF NATURAL JUSTICE NOT WARRANTED

As mentioned earlier, affording reasonable opportunity of being heard is an essential component of quasi-judicial proceedings. At the same time, the defendant should not be allowed to make a fraud on the above provisions by seeking unreasonable number of opportunities with the *malafide* intention of prolonging the inquiry unnecessarily, ostensibly to evade his liability under the statute. Justice V.R.Krishna Iyer, in the case of *The Chairman, Board of Mining Examination and Chief*

32

Inspector of Mines, and Ors. vs. Ramjee brilliantly described that natural justice is no unruly horse, no lurking land mine, nor a judicial cure-all. If fairness is shown by the decision-maker to the man proceeded against, the form, features and the fundamentals of such essential processual propriety being conditioned by the facts and circumstances of each situation, no breach of natural justice can be complained of. Unnatural expansion of natural justice, without reference to the administrative realities and other factors of a given case, can be exasperating. We can neither be finical nor firm in this jurisdiction. No man shall be hit below the belt -- that is the conscience of the matter.

The Hon'ble Apex Court in its Larger Bench decision in the case of *Managing Director, ECIL vs. B. Karunakar*[28], has observed that when the employee is dismissed or removed from service and the inquiry is set aside because the report is not furnished to him, in some cases the non-furnishing of the report may have prejudiced him gravely while in other cases it may have made no difference to the ultimate punishment awarded to him. The theory of reasonable opportunity and the principles of natural justice have been evolved to uphold the rule of law and to assist the individual to vindicate his just rights. They are neither incantations to be invoked nor rites to be performed on all and sundry occasions. Whether, in fact, prejudice has been caused to the employee or not on account of the denial to him of the report, has to be considered on the facts and circumstances of each case. Where, therefore, even after the furnishing of the report, no different consequence would have followed, it would be a perversion of justice to permit the employee to resume duty and to get all the consequential benefits. It amounts to rewarding the dishonest and the guilty and thus to stretching the concept of justice to illogical and exasperating limits. It amounts to an *'unnatural expansion of natural justice'* which in itself is antithetical to justice.

---

[28] AIR 1994 SC 1075

NATURAL JUSTICE UNDER EXCEPTIONAL CIRCUMSTANCES

In the case of *Bharat Barrel & Drum Manufacturing Co. vs L.K.Bose*[29] it has been held that rules of natural justice are not inflexible rules or of universal application. Court has to consider in each case whether, in the light of the facts and circumstances of the case, the nature of issues involved in an enquiry, the nature of the order passed and interest affected thereby, a fair and reasonable opportunity of being heard was furnished to the person affected.

This position was reiterated by the Supreme Court in the case of *Union of India vs J.N.Sinha*[30] that the rules of natural justice are neither embodied rules nor can they be elevated to the position of fundamental rights. Their aim is to secure justice or to prevent miscarriage of justice. These rules can operate only in areas not covered by any law validly made. They do not supplant the law but supplement it. If a statutory provision can be read consistently with the principles of natural justice, the courts should do so. But, if a statutory provision either specifically or by necessary implication excludes the application of any rules of natural justice, then the court cannot ignore the mandate of the legislature or the statutory authority and read into the concerned provision the principles of natural justice. Whether the exercise of a power conferred should be made in accordance with any of the principles of natural justice or not depends upon the express words of the provision conferring the power, the nature of the power conferred, the purpose for which it is conferred and the effect of the exercise of that power.

In *Hira Nath vs Rajendra Medical College, Ranchi*, the appellants were male students of the Respondent College who had been expelled from the college for having entered the Girls' hostel naked and tried to pull the hands of a girl student in the hostel. The appellants challenged the order of expulsion on the ground that the statements of the girl students were recorded behind the back of the appellants and the former were not allowed to be cross-examined.

---

[29] AIR 1967 SC 361
[30] AIR 1971 SC 40

In rejecting these contentions, the court said that the requirements of natural justice did not remain the same under all circumstances. These findings of the Supreme Court should have been rested on the principle laid down by the House of Lords in *In re.K(Infants)*[31] namely that the principles of Natural Justice are intended to serve the ends of Justice. If it can be shown that any of the principles will not serve the ends of Justice, 'it must be dismissed,' for otherwise the servant becomes the master or the means becomes an end". (*H.M.Seervai, 1984*)

---

[31] 1965 AC 201

CHAPTER 3
ELEMENTS OF A FAIR QUASI-JUDICIAL PROCEEDINGS

Because 'the *due process*' condition applies to quasi-judicial matters, quasi-judicial hearings are very formal and procedural. However, they should not be as formal as a court proceeding. One should keep in mind that quasi-judicial decisions may be overturned by a court if proper procedures are not followed, even if the decision itself is a *'correct'* one. Procedural due process requirements are similar to a recipe for baking a cake. The cake does not suddenly appear – it is made only after each step of the recipe is followed closely. If the baker leaves out one ingredient or adds too much of another, the results can be disastrous. (Hunter, 2009) Thus, it is important to scrupulously follow the procedural formalities while conducting a quasi-judicial hearing.

(1) ADEQUATE NOTICE

As we noted earlier, the principles of natural justice require that the defendants should be given adequate notice of the allegations against him and of the procedure for deciding on the issues so that he may be in a position to make representations on his behalf, to appear at the hearing to effectively present his case. The term *'notice'* originated from the Latin word *'Notitia'* which means 'being known'. The parties to the proceedings should get adequate notice and an adequate effective opportunity to defend themselves. The date, time and place of the hearing must be notified in advance to the defendants and other interested parties. The notice should also include a reference to the statutes and rules involved, and a short, plain statement of the facts alleged.

The test of the adequacy of the notice will be whether it gives the sufficient information and material so as to enable the person concerned to prepare for his defence. There should also be sufficient time to comply with the requirements of a notice. Notably, a person cannot be punished for the charges which were not mentioned in the notice.

When the defendant fails to appear for the inquiry without assigning any reasons, the Inquiry Officer has discretion how to proceed further – whether to give one more opportunity or to decide the matter *ex parte* based on the available records. Before deciding this, he should confirm that the summons/notice was served upon the defendant and he was aware of the time and place for the hearing and whether the time allowed is so reasonable that he could have appeared without difficulty.

(2) IMPARTIAL HEARING OFFICER

The persons who conduct quasi-judicial hearings are expected to perform a presiding function similar to that of a judge. Judges, like Caesar's wife, should be above suspicion. He must have no pecuniary or proprietary interest in the outcome of the proceedings.

Bias or prejudice vitiates all quasi-judicial proceedings rendering them a nullity. A bias is an unreasonable favour or disfavour, usually in the sense for having a preference to one particular point of view or ideological perspective. *Prejudice* is, as the name implies[32], the process of 'pre-judging' something. A decision which is a result of bias is a nullity and the trial is '*Coram non judice*', a legal term typically used to indicate a legal proceeding held 'without a judge', or without proper jurisdiction.

Bias can take many forms: Personal bias, pecuniary bias, subject-matter bias, departmental bias or official bias, pre-conceived notion bias or prejudice.

In the case of *A.K.Kraipak vs Union of India*[33], Naquishband who was the acting Chief Conservator of Forests, was a member of the Selection Board and was also a candidate for selection to All-India Cadre of the Indian Forest Service. Though he did not take part in the deliberations of the Board when his name was considered and approved, the Supreme Court of India held that 'there was a real likelihood of a bias for the mere

---

[32] from *præ*-'before' + *judicium* 'judgment'
[33] AIR 1970 SC 150

presence of the candidate on the Selection Board may adversely influence the judgement of the other members.'

Doctrine of Necessity

The doctrine of necessity is an exception to the principle of bias, that is, no man shall be a judge in his own case.

The question whether the selection of a candidate who happens to be a close relative of a member of Public Service Commission get vitiated for bias came before the judicial scrutiny of the Supreme Court in the case of *Ashok Kumar Yadav vs State of Haryana*[34]. Under ordinary circumstances, the entire selection process would get vitiated on account of *'reasonable likelihood of bias'* affecting the process of selection. But this is not applicable in the case of a member of the Union or State Public Service Commission which is a constitutional body. This is so because if a member decides to withdraw himself from the entire selection process, there could be no immediate substitute to clear the vacuum. In such case, it is desirable that the member must withdraw from the participation of interview of the known candidate and he should also not take part in the discussions. The Supreme Court conceptualized the 'doctrine of necessity' in this case.

In the case of *J. Mohapatra & Co And Another vs State Of Orissa And Another*[35] the Supreme Court observed,

'The doctrine of necessity is however, an exception to the doctrine of bias, that no man shall be a judge in his own cause. An adjudicator, who is subject to disqualification on the ground of bias or interest in the matter which he has to decide, may be required to adjudicate if there is no other person who is competent or authorized to adjudicate or if a quorum cannot be formed without him or if no other competent tribunal can be constituted. In such cases, the principle of natural justice would have to give way to necessity for otherwise there would be no means of deciding the matter and the machinery of justice or administration would break

---

[34] 1987 AIR 454, 1985 SCR Supl. (1) 657
[35] 1984 AIR 1572, 1985 SCR (1) 322

down' Thus, in *The Judges vs. Attorney-General* for Saskatchewan[36], the Judges of the Court of Appeal were held competent to decide the question whether Judges of the Court of Appeal, of the Court of King's Bench and of the District Courts of the Province of Saskatchewan were subject to taxation under the Income-tax Act, 1932, of Saskatchewan on the ground that they were bound to act ex-necessitate. The doctrine of necessity applies not only to judicial matters but also to quasi-judicial and administrative matters.

(3) RIGHT TO BE REPRESENTED BY OR THROUGH A COUNSEL

Proceedings before a quasi-judicial agency ought not to be equated with proceedings before a court of law. As a matter of practice and policy, legal representations are not considered in cases not involving complex legal and factual issues. However, where the person is illiterate, or the matter is technical and expertise is needed to deal with the case, or when a expert evidence is on record, or where a substantial question of law is involved, or when a person is required to face a trained legal practitioner during the course of the proceedings, he may be permitted to engage a legal counsel of choice. For instance, Section 36 of the Industrial Disputes Act 1947 makes the consent of the other party and the leave of the court the prerequisites before an advocate can represent a party in the labour court[37].

Thus, the right to be represented through a counsel is not a part of the principles of natural justice. The Supreme Court in the *Bharat Petroleum Corporation Ltd vs. Maharashtra General Kamgar Union*[38] held that a delinquent employee has no right to be represented by an advocate in the departmental proceedings and that if a right to be represented by a co-workman is given to him, the departmental proceedings would not be bad only for the reason that the assistance of an advocate was not provided to him.

---

[36] (1937)53 Times Law Reporter 464:

[37] A lawyer can however appear before the Labour Court in the capacity of an office-bearer of a Labour Union or a head of an Association representing the workers.

[38] (1993) 2 SCC 115

(4) RIGHT TO CONFRONT PARTIES AND WITNESSES

The Indian judicial system itself is based on the *adversary system* of justice, which is contra-distinct to the *inquisitorial system*. H.W.R.Wade and C.F.Forsyth in their *'Administrative Law' (8th Edition)* describe 'adversary procedure' as follows:

'It is fundamental that the procedure before a tribunal, like that in a court of law, should be adversary and not inquisitorial. The tribunal should have both sides of the case presented to it and should judge between them, without itself having to conduct an inquiry of its own motion, enter into the controversy and call evidence for or against either party. It if allows itself to become involved in the investigation and argument, parties will quickly lose confidence in its impartiality, however fair-minded it may be. This principle is observed throughout the tribunal system.'

As distinct from the adversary system, the inquisitorial system will empower the quasi-judicial authority further with the duty of leading evidence with the objective of seeking the truth.

Thus, the quasi-judicial system in India, having adopted the adversary system of functioning[39], has to rely upon examination and cross-examination of parties and witnesses.

The right to confront parties and witnesses include, among other things, (i) the opportunity to introduce evidence and otherwise be heard on the party's own behalf; (ii) the right to confront or meet face to face witnesses testifying against him and to cross-examine them; and (iii) admit or deny the allegations against the party in the petition. They also have the right to be physically present in the Court room when witnesses are testifying against them. Another derivative benefit of this right is to make the adjudicator to see for himself the manner by which the witnesses

---

[39] There are some exceptions to this. In the case *of Uttarpara Children's Own Home vs Union of India*, Kolkata High Court held that quasi-judicial proceedings under Section 7A of the Employees' Provident Funds and Miscellaneous Provisions Act 1952 are essentially inquisitorial and not adversarial.

testify in the court, their reaction during the cross-examination and to test the believability of a witness and the truth of his testimony.

It may however be noted that cross-examination of the witnesses is not an obligatory part of natural justice and depends upon the circumstances of the case and the nature of the statute under which hearing is held. In the case of *State of Jammu and Kashmir vs. Bakshii Ghulam Mohd*[40], the Government of Jammu and Kashmir appointed a Commissioner of Inquiry to inquire into the charges of corruption and maladministration against the ex-Chief Minister of the State. He claimed the right to cross-examine the witnesses on the grounds of natural justice. The Court interpreted the statute and held that only those witnesses who deposed orally against the ex-Chief Minister can be cross-examined and not of those who merely filed affidavits.

(5) RIGHT TO COMPEL PRODUCTION OF EVIDENCE

When the institution/body/organization has the power to subpoena[41] witnesses and records, the party whose rights are to be decided in the inquiry, must have a similar right to use the subpoena for the production of witnesses and evidences in support of their cause.

Noting that Section 7-A of the Employees' Provident Funds and Miscellaneous Provisions Act authorized the Commissioner to enforce attendance, to examine on oath and to require discovery and production of documents, the Supreme Court observed:

'The question is not whether one had failed to produce evidence. The question is whether the Commissioner who is the statutory authority had exercised powers vested in him to collect the relevant evidence before determining the amount payable under the said Act.... The Commissioner should exercise all his powers to collect the evidence and collate all material before coming to proper conclusion. That is the legal duty of the Commissioner. It would be failure to exercise the jurisdiction particularly when a

---

[40] 1967 AIR 122, 1966 SCR (4) 1
[41] A writ requiring appearance in court to give testimony

party to the proceedings requests for summoning evidence from a particular person'[*Food Corporation of India vs. Regional Provident Fund Commissioner*[42]],The Supreme Court, in the *State of Bombay vs. Nurul Latif Khan*[43], has observed that if the defendant desires to examine witnesses whose evidence appears to the Inquiry Officer completely irrelevant, the Inquiry Officer may refuse to examine such witnesses but in doing so he will have to record his special and sufficient reasons".

(6) RIGHT TO HAVE FINDINGS OF FACTS AND LAW, AND EXPLICIT REASONS FOR THE DECISION (SPEAKING ORDER)

While adjudicating the issues, the quasi-judicial authority ought to appreciate the entire record and evidences, and not just to evidence that is favourable to the appellant or isolated from a consideration of the record as a whole.

The expression 'speaking order' was first coined by Lord Chancellor Earl Cairns (in a rather strange context than we use it today) in *Overseers of the Poor of Walsall vs London and North Eastern Railway Co (1878) 4 AC .35 P.39* . The Lord Chancellor, while explaining the ambit of Writ of Certiorari, referred to orders with errors on the face of the record and pointed out that an order with errors on its face is a '*speaking order.*'

The principle of natural justice demands that justice must not only be done, but it must eminently appear to be done. The essential of a speaking order is the reason underlying the making of the order is manifestly evident on the fact of it, and needs no additional explanation. It flows from the judicial maxim '*Ces-sante Ratione Legis Cessat Ipsa Lex*' which means 'reason is the soul of law, and when the reason of any particular law ceases, so does the law itself.'

---

[42] (1990) 1 SCC 68: 1990 SCC (L&S)1: (1990) 1 Cur LR 20

[43] AIR 1966 SC 269

A non-speaking order is virtually no order in the eyes of law. Absence of reasons in the original order cannot be compensated by disclosure of reasons in the appellate order.

Judiciary deems 'speaking order' an integral part of principles of natural justice and an essential attribute of quasi-judicial orders. The Supreme Court of India has laid down in *Maharashtra S.B vs .Gandhi*[44] that every judicial and quasi-judicial authority must record reasons for its decision. If no decisions are given, the supervisory jurisdiction would become nugatory. In another case, it held that when an authority, be it administrative, or quasi-judicial, adjudicates a dispute, and if its order is appealable or subject to judicial review, it is necessary for the authority to spell out its reasons for passing an order.

If the order speaks only with the 'inscrutable face of a sphinx,' it would be impossible for the High Courts and Supreme Court to effectively exercise their power of judicial review by means of Certiorari [*Testeels Ltd. vs Desai (N.M)*,][45]

Summarizing many of the case laws, the Supreme Court in the case of *M/s Kranti Asso. Pvt. Ltd. & Anr. vs Masood Ahmed Khan & Ors*[46]., held that,

(i)   In India, the judicial trend has always been to record reasons, even in administrative decisions, if such decisions affect anyone prejudicially.

(ii)   A quasi-judicial authority must record reasons in support of its conclusions.

(iii) Insistence on recording of reason is meant to serve the wider principle of justice that justice must not only be done; it must appear to be done as well.

(iv)   Recording of reasons also operates as a valid restraint on any possible arbitrary exercise of judicial and quasi-judicial or even administrative power.

---

[44] (1991) 2 S.C.C. 716
[45] 1970(20)FLR121, (1969)10 GLR 622, (1970)I LLJ 210 Guj
[46] (2010) 9 SCC 496]

(v)   Reasons reassure that discretion has been exercised by the decision maker on relevant grounds and by disregarding extraneous considerations.

(vi)   Reasons have virtually become as indispensable a component of a decision making process as observing principles of natural justice by judicial, quasi-judicial and even by administrative bodies.

(iv)   Reasons facilitate the process of judicial review by superior Courts.

(v)   The ongoing judicial trend in all countries committed to rule of law and constitutional governance is in favour of reasoned decisions based on relevant facts. This is virtually the life blood of judicial decision making justifying the principle that reason is the soul of justice.

(vi)   Judicial or even quasi-judicial opinions these days can be as different as the judges and authorities who deliver them. All these decisions serve one common purpose which is to demonstrate by reason that the relevant factors have been objectively considered. This is important for sustaining the litigants' faith in the justice delivery system.

(vii) Insistence on reason is a requirement for both judicial accountability and transparency.

(viii) If a Judge or a quasi-judicial authority is not candid enough about his/her decision making process then it is impossible to know whether the person deciding is faithful to the doctrine of precedent or to [the] principles of incrementalism.

(ix)   Reasons in support of decisions must be cogent, clear and succinct. A pretence of reasons or 'rubber-stamp reasons' is not to be equated with a valid decision making process.

(x)   It cannot be doubted that transparency is the *sine qua non* of restraint on abuse of judicial powers. Transparency in decision making not only makes the judges and decision makers less prone to errors but also makes them subject to broader scrutiny[See *David Shapiro in Defence of Judicial Candor* (1987) 100 Harward Law Review 731-737]

(xi) Since the requirements to record reasons emanates from the broad doctrine of fairness in decision making, the said requirement is now virtually a component of human rights and was considered part of Strasbourg Jurisprudence [See (1994) 19 EHRR 553, at 562 Para 29 and Anya vs. University of Oxford, 2001 EWCA Civ 405, wherein the Court referred to Article 6 of European Convention of Human Rights which requires, 'adequate and intelligent reasons must be given for judicial decisions.']

(xii) In all common law jurisdictions, judgements play a vital role in setting up precedents for the future. Therefore, for development of law, requirement of giving reasons for the decision is of the essence and is virtually a part of '*due process.*'

Though it is important that the order should contain reasons, it is equally important to mention here that the authority is not bound to explain, clarify or interpret his findings at a later stage, apart from those enumerated in his order. The Supreme Court of India, in the case of *Khanapuram Gandaiah vs. Administrative Officer and Others* [47] held as follows:

'A judge speaks through his judgments or orders passed by him. If any party feels aggrieved by the order/judgment passed by a judge, the remedy available to such a party is either to challenge the same by way of appeal or by revision, or any other legally permissible mode. No litigant can be allowed to seek information as to why and for what reasons the judge had come to a particular decision or conclusion. A judge is not bound to explain later on for what reasons he had come to such a conclusion.'

---

[47] SLP(Civil) No.34868 of 2009, Order dated January 4, 2010

Mere fact that the proceedings were treated as confidential does not dispense with the requirement of recording reasons.[*Harinagar Sugar Mills vs. Shyam Sunder*][48]

If the reasons recorded are totally irrelevant, the exercise of power would be bad and the order is liable to be set aside [*M/s Hochtief Gammon vs. State of Orissa*][49]

The validity of the order passed by the statutory authority must be judged by the reasons recorded therein and cannot be construed in the light of subsequent explanations given by the authority concerned or filing affidavit. Orders are not like old wine becoming better as they grow older [*Mohinder Singh Gill vs. Chief Election Commissioner*][50].

(7) RIGHT TO JUDICIAL REVIEW OF ADMINISTRATIVE DECISIONS

Appeals of quasi-judicial authorities are reviewed by superior Courts in the nature of certiorari and prohibition. Judicial review is meant to ensure a minimal threshold required to preserve the validity of a quasi-judicial decision, especially in a Parliamentary form of government like ours and where the concept of 'judicial review' forms the basic structure of the constitution.

The judicial review is to consider, but not necessarily bound by, the interpretations of the quasi-judicial authority and may consider whether the impugned order suffers from any violations of the constitutional provisions, excess of statutory authority, inconsistent with the established procedure, affected by error of law, unsupported by substantial and competent evidences on record, and arbitrary or capricious.

---

[48] AIR 1961 SC 1669 (1678, 1683).
[49] (1975) 2 SCO 649 : AIR 1975 SC 2226
[50] (1978) 1 SCC 405 (417) : AIR 1978 SC 851 (858)

CHAPTER 4
NATURE OF QUASI-JUDICIAL FUNCTIONS

Originally, adjudication was a subject matter falling within the exclusive domain of courts. This was in line with the principle of separation of powers, that is, the idea of government as a trio of branches – legislative, executive and judicial. Over the years, the phenomenal increase in the workload of judicial courts and the evolving complexities of matters of adjudication necessitated the emergence of quasi-judicial bodies. Administrative Tribunals/quasi-judicial agencies have emerged not only in India but also in many other countries with the objective of providing a new type of justice – public good oriented justice. According to Hood Phillips and Jackson, 'the reasons why Parliament increasingly confers powers of adjudication on special tribunals rather than on the ordinary courts may be stated positively as showing the greater suitability of such tribunals, or negatively as showing the inadequacy of the ordinary courts for the particular kind of work that has to be done.' (Jackson, 2001)

They are not bound by the elaborate rules of evidence or procedures governing the ordinary courts of law. Judicial power was delegated to administrative bodies/tribunals mainly to lessen the burden of Court, to impart the necessary expertise into the process of adjudication and to provide cheap, easily accessible, informal and speedy justice to the citizenry. Again, since the judicial functions are discharged by administrative bodies, it becomes more important that the procedures are strictly regulated to ensure discharge of quasi-judicial functions in a just and fair manner and that injustice is not done to any party.

NOT A CASE OF APPEAL FROM CAESAR TO CAESAR

A particularly perplexing problem is presented when the department (whose employee the inquiry officers happens to be often) is itself a party to the issue to be decided – to sit in judgment in its own case. It is often said that the hearing to be given to the person before the Inquiry Officer of a department would be almost like '*an appeal from Caesar to Caesar.*' But the facts are different. The authority envisaged under the statutes are required to objectively decide the issues based on the given facts and materials on record. He himself is not a party as such to the issue that the statute calls upon him to decide and, while deciding such issue, he himself does not act as a judge in his own cause. To say that no one shall be a judge in his own cause means that the judge must not have anything like personal interest in the cause he is to adjudicate upon and not that an officer discharging his official functions himself should not start proceedings in a manner which he is always competent to do under the law. In deciding a matter quasi-judicially, the decision of the authority is not to be influenced by the departmental instructions – rather he is to go by his own best judgment [*Rajagopala Naidi vs. State Transport Appellate Tribunal[51]*]. The mere fact that a body/institution/organization is a party to a dispute before it is not alone an indication of bias sufficient to violate due process of law.

QUASI-JUDICIAL POWERS CANNOT BE DELEGATED

Practically, Inquiry Officers under various statutes perform both administrative and judicial functions. Legally, they can delegate to others their administrative functions but not judicial functions. The very object of conferring quasi-judicial powers on an administrative authority is that entrusted powers must be exercised by that authority only and it cannot be sub-delegated to any other authority.

As held by the Supreme Court in *Bombay Municipal Corpn. vs. Dhondu Narayan Chowdhary[52]*, it is well settled that judicial power cannot ordinarily be delegated unless the law expressly or by clear implication, permits it. Why the quasi-judicial functions should not be delegated? The basic tenet of delegation is that 'a delegated authority cannot delegate further' [*Deligatus non protest delegare*]. Judicial power is originally vested in the judiciary. Quasi-judicial power is a derivative, a result of valid delegation of judicial powers to administrative bodies. Thus quasi-judicial powers, being delegated powers, cannot be delegated again.

---

[51] AIR 1964 SC 1573
[52] AIR 1965 SC 1486

QUASI-JUDICIAL FUNCTIONARIES CANNOT CHALLENGE ORDERS OF THE APPELLATE AUTHORITY

In some occasions, orders passed by the quasi-judicial authorities come up for scrutiny before Appellate Authority who also happens to be a quasi-judicial authority. For instance, quasi-judicial orders passed under Section 7A of the Employees' Provident Funds and Miscellaneous Provisions Act, 1952 are appealable before the Employees' Provident Funds Appellate Tribunal instituted under Section 7-I of the said Act. When a Section 7A order is challenged before the Tribunal, it has many options. It can nullify the order or remand it for reconsideration by the officer who passed it. Alternatively, the Tribunal can also sit for adjudication and conduct *de novo* inquiry by itself, for like a Regional Provident Fund Commissioner, or an Assistant Provident Fund Commissioner, *the EPF Appellate Tribunal is also empowered to conduct inquiry under Section 7A of the Act.*

Naturally then a question arises: If a quasi-judicial order passed under Section 7A of the Act is overturned by the Appellate Tribunal, can the inquiry officer who passed the impugned order challenge the Tribunal order by way of a Writ? Many judicial pronouncements say he cannot.

In *Regional Provident Fund Commissioner, Tirunelveli v. Prabha Beverages Pvt. Ltd.*, a learned single Judge of the Madras High Court considered the question whether the Regional Provident Fund Commissioner who had passed the assessment order under section 7A of the Act is competent to maintain a writ petition challenging the order of the Employees Provident Fund Appellate Tribunal which interfered with the said order. Relying on the decision of the Apex Court in *Union Of India v. K.M.Sankarappa*[53] and the decision of the Division Bench of the Madras High Court in *Central Board of Film Certification v. Yadavalaya Films*[54] the learned Judge held that the Regional Provident Fund Commissioner is not competent to maintain the writ petition, The principle that

---

[53] AIR 2000 SC 3678
[54] 2007 (2) MLJ 604

emerges from the decisions referred to above is that an adjudicating authority which exercises quasi-judicial powers and discharges quasi- judicial functions cannot in the absence of any specific conferment of power, challenge an order passed by the Appellate Authority, since it would be subversive of judicial discipline.

DOCTRINE OF ABSOLUTE QUASI-JUDICIAL IMMUNITY

Absolute immunity is extended to government officials who perform quasi-judicial functions. It protects the quasi-judicial officers from legal action for wrongs committed by them when acting that capacity.

Not all actions of the quasi-judicial authorities are protected by absolute immunity. The doctrine of absolute immunity applies according to the motives of the quasi-judicial officer. In case he had ulterior *malafide* motives and acted intentionally and maliciously, then the immunity is not available to him to save his skin.

The Supreme Court, in the case of *Ramesh Chander Singh vs High Court of Allahabad and another*[55] has observed as follows: - 'In *Zunjarrao Bhikaji Nagarkar v. Union of India*, this Court held that wrong exercise of jurisdiction by a quasi-judicial authority or mistake of law or wrong interpretation of law cannot be the basis for initiating disciplinary proceedings.'

The Supreme Court in *P.C.Joshi vs. State of U.P and Others*[56], while referring to the law laid down in *A.N.Sexana's* case[57] and *K.K.Dhawan's* case[58] to the effect that disciplinary action can be initiated in respect of judicial or quasi-judicial order under certain contingencies, quashed the ultimate punishment on the basis of factual finding that there was no allegation nor any proof of any recklessness or misconduct in duty.

---

[55] (2007) 4 SCC 247
[56] (2001) 6 SCC 491
[57] (1992) 3 SCC 124
[58] (1993) 2 SCC 56

In the case of *E.S.Sanjeeva Rao vs.Central Bureau of Investigation and ors*[59], the Hon'ble High Court of Bombay held that (i) the Regional Provident Fund Commissioner, performing quasi-judicial functions under Section 7A of the Employees' Provident Funds and Miscellaneous Provisions Act 1952 is a 'judge' within the meaning of Section 19 of the Indian Penal Code and Section 2 of the Judges (Protection) Act, 1985. (ii) The calculation of dues made by the Central Bureau of Investigation while framing charges on the Commissioner cannot constitute an offence (as it constitute hypothetical calculation made by the CBI as if sitting in appeal over the order passed by the Regional PF Commissioner) and (iii) the prosecution of the Regional Provident Fund Commissioner only on the basis of Section 77 of the Indian Penal Code or Section 3(1) of the Judges (Protection) Act, 1985 is barred by law.

The Supreme Court of India has held that disciplinary action can be taken against quasi-judicial officers under the following instances:

(i)   Where the officer had acted in a manner as would reflect on his reputation for integrity or good faith or devotion to duty

(ii) If there is prima facie material to show recklessness or misconduct in the discharge of his duty

(iii) If he has acted in a manner which is unbecoming of a Government servant

(iv) If he had acted negligently or that he omitted the prescribed conditions which are essential for the exercise of the statutory powers

(v)   If he had acted in order to unduly favour a party

(vi) If he had been actuated by corrupt motive, however small the bribe may be because Lord Coke said long ago *'though the bribe maybe small, yet the fault is great.'*

---

[59] W.P (Crl) No.2637 of 2010

NEGLIGENT/RECKLESS OFFICERS SUSCEPTIBLE FOR DISCIPLINARY ACTION

Quasi-judicial powers need to be exercised with diligence and due care. The freedom, liberty and power given to the authority to decide an issue cannot be taken as a licence to act in a reckless manner. Power does not justify acts of negligence.

The Supreme Court of India, in the case of *Union of India and others vs. Duli Chand*[60] went to the extent of decreeing that when an officer who exercised quasi-judicial powers, acting negligently or recklessly could be proceeded against by way of disciplinary action.

In *Govinda Menon vs. Union of India*[61] it was contended that no disciplinary proceedings could be taken against appellant for acts or omissions with regard to his work as Commissioner under Madras Hindu Religious and Charitable Endowments Act, 1951. Since the orders made by him were quasi-judicial in character, they should be challenged only as provided for under the Act. It was further contended that having regard to scope of Rule 4 of All India Services(Discipline and Appeal) Rules, 1955, the act or omission of the Commissioner was such that appellant was not subject to the administrative control of the Government and therefore, the disciplinary proceedings were void. Rejecting this contention it was held as under:

'It is not disputed that the appropriate Government has power to take disciplinary proceedings against the appellant and that he could be removed from service by an order of the Central Government, but it was contended that I.A.S Officers are governed by statutory rules, that, any act or omission referred to in Rule 4(1) relates only to an act or omission of an officer when serving under the Government, and that "serving under the Government" means subject to the administrative control of the Government and that disciplinary proceedings should be, therefore, on the basis of the relationship of master and servant. It was argued that in exercising statutory powers the Commissioner was not subject to the

---

[60] 2006(5)SCC 680
[61] 1967 SC 1274

administrative control of the Government and disciplinary proceedings cannot, therefore, be instituted against the appellant in respect of an act or omission committed by him in the course of his employment as Commissioner. We are unable to accept the proposition contended for by the appellant as correct. Rule 4(1) does not impose any limitation or qualification as to the nature of the act or omission in respect of which disciplinary proceedings can be instituted.'

Disciplinary action against quasi-judicial officers can be taken on the grounds of incompetency, dishonesty, discourteous behaviour, engaging in private employment inconsistent with official duties and so on.

REVIEW POWER OF QUASI-JUDICIAL AUTHORITIES

It is well established principle that an administrative authority has the power to review its orders. The provisions of Section 21 of the General Clauses Act confer ample jurisdiction on an administrative authority to amend, vary or rescind its orders. In case of a quasi-judicial officer, there is no inherent power to review his earlier order on the question of law, unless so empowered expressly or impliedly by an Act or rules.

In *DrSmtKuntesh Gupta vs. Management of Hindu Kanya Mahavidyalaya Sitapur (U.P) and Ors.*,[62] the Supreme Court was considering a case where Vice-Chancellor had no power to review under the statutes of the University or under the U.P. State University Act, 1973. In that situation, it was held, 'It is now well established that a quasi-judicial authority cannot review its own order, unless the power of review is expressly conferred on it by the statute under which it derives its jurisdiction. The Vice-Chancellor in considering the question of approval of an order of dismissal of the principal acts as a quasi judicial authority. It is not disputed that the provisions of the U. P. State Universities Act, 1973 or of the Statutes of the University do not confer any power of review on the Vice-Chancellor. In the circumstances, it must be held that the Vice-Chancellor acted wholly without jurisdiction in reviewing her order.'

---

[62] 1987 AIR 2186, 1988 SCR (1) 357

The question whether the Employees' Provident Funds Appellate Tribunal has an inherent power to review its own order come under judicial scrutiny in the case of *A.L.Kapur & Other vs. Presiding Officer, EPF Appellate Tribunal & Others* (W.P.No.1068 of 1998).

In the said case, the Presiding Officer of the EPF Appellate Tribunal wanted to review his own order on the pretext of many typographical errors and other things. The petitioner raised a preliminary objection stating that there were no typographical errors and the EPFAT in fact wanted to review its own order and reverse the same without any basis. He contested that the Tribunal has not the power to review its own order. Section 7L of the Employees' Provident Funds and Miscellaneous Provisions Act 1952 which confers power on the Appellate Tribunal to correct mistakes, cannot be used to review its own order by the EPF Appellate Tribunal.

Supreme Court has categorically laid down that review of its own order by a quasi-judicial Tribunal is permissible only where there is a procedural mistake or procedural illegality i.e., a mistake of the nature which vitiated the proceedings itself and consequently the award. However, the Tribunal has no power to review its order on merits unless power of review is expressly conferred on it by the statute under which it derives its jurisdiction.

The Apex Court again clarified this position in *Rajender Singh vs. Lt.Governor, Andaman & Nicobar Islands & Ors* [63] 'The power, in our opinion, extends to correct all errors to prevent miscarriage of justice. The courts should not hesitate to review its own earlier order when there exists an error on the face of the record and the interest of the justice so demands in appropriate cases.'

QUASI-JUDICIAL FORUM CANNOT BE OVERLOOKED

If there is an alternative remedy instituted in the statute itself, the aggrieved person should exhaust it before invoking the extraordinary provisions of Writ, because it is a discretionary remedy of the Court.

---

[63] AIR 2006 SC 75

The Supreme Court held that when there has been a special enactment, which provides for an obligation for remedy, the parties will have to avail that remedy at the first instance and the remedy under Article 226 of the Constitution will not be available. (*Rajkumar Shivhare vs Assistant Director, Directorate of Enforcement and another*[64]).

QUASI-JUDICIAL OFFICER NOT BOUND BY ADVICE OF OTHERS

The President of India and Governors of States, though act according to the advice rendered by the Council of Ministers, are required to act judicially under certain circumstances. For instance, under Article 217(3) of the Indian Constitution, the President of India is the adjudicating authority to determine the age of a Judge of the High Court. It has been held that while exercising the powers conferred by Article 217(3), the President discharges a judicial function and is not required to act on the advice of the Council of Ministers; his only obligation being to decide the question about the age of the Judge after consulting the Chief Justice of India (*Union of India vs. Jyoti Prakash.Mitter*[65]). Though the quasi-judicial functionaries can consult others, the final discretion to accept or not to accept such advice rests with them only.

---

[64] (2010) 4 SCC 772
[65] 1971 AIR 1093, 1971 SCR (3) 483

CHAPTER 5
CONDUCTING OF QUASI-JUDICIAL PROCEEDINGS

Since a quasi-judicial hearing has many features of a court trial, the procedures in such hearing are governed by the constitutional requirements of due process, which calls for general procedural fairness.

Again, there is a remarkable difference between a court trial and a quasi-judicial hearing. While the general procedural rules do apply in both the cases, those relating to rules of evidence [what evidence is admissible and what is not] differ as they relate to quasi-judicial hearings, depending upon the nature of the issues to be adjudicated. Formal rules of evidence are not adopted, but a well-established hearing protocol is essential.

DECORUM OF PROCEEDINGS

Quasi-judicial proceedings are serious in nature and all parties to the proceedings are supposed to act in a courteous and respectful manner. The officer conducting quasi-judicial proceedings should act like a 'judge' and treat the process a 'judicial' one. Hearing needs to be held in a quiet and orderly setting. Crowding can create an unreceptive atmosphere. Loud, rude or disruptive behaviour, or outbursts, loss of temperament, in support of or opposition to statements made by others will not be tolerated by the Chairperson. Cellular phones and other communication devices must be placed in silent-mode prior to entering the hearing room to prevent inappropriate ringing. Proper conduct must be maintained at all times.

The Inquiry Officer should be adequately prepared for conduction of the hearing. In many of the quasi-judicial proceedings, it is likely that there will be only one party before the hearing officer. An inquiry officer under Section 7A of the Employees' Provident Funds and Miscellaneous Provisions Act, 1952 will hear only the employer usually [though some administrative instructions require the Inspector to be present to represent the cause of the department]. In such cases, the inquiry officer cannot make use of the *'adversary processes'* [which is used by the judicial courts] – the arguments between a plaintiff and a defendant – to bring out the full facts of the case.

The Inquiry Officer therefore ought to be thoroughly acquainted with the facts of the case and the provisions, rules and regulations relevant to it. He should come to the case with an open mind without preconceived notions of the outcome. He must perform his quasi-judicial duties impartially and fairly. Facial expression and body language as well his language can give to parties in the proceedings an appearance of official bias. He should therefore be alert to avoid even behaviours that may be perceived as prejudicial.

DRESS CODE

Dress code is a part of the court etiquette and forms important complement to the standards of quasi-judicial proceedings. In many a case, the rules regulating the quasi-judicial functions themselves prescribe dress code for the Inquiry Officer and the parties who appear before him. For instance, Rules 26 and 27 of the Employees' Provident Funds Appellate Tribunal (Procedure) Rules, 1997 provides for dress code of the Presiding Officer and his Staff as well as for the parties. Dress code for the Presiding Officer and his Staffs will be specified by the former. For the parties, they may wear their professional dress, if any, and if there is no such dress, a male member needs to be in a closed collared coat and trousers or in a lounge suit. Female members may be in a sari, or any other customary dress of sober colour.

Similarly, the Council of the Institute of Company Secretaries of India has prescribed the following guidelines for professional dress for its members while appearing before quasi-judicial bodies and tribunals.

1. The professional dress for male members will be navy blue suit and white shirt with a tie or navy blue buttoned-up coat over a pant or a navy blue safari suit.

2. The professional dress for female members will be sari or any other dress of a sober colour with a navy blue jacket.

3. Members in employment may wear the dress/uniform as specified by the employer for all employees, or if allowed the aforesaid professional dress.

4. Practicing Company Secretaries appearing before any tribunal or quasi-judicial body should adhere to dress code if any prescribed for appearing before such tribunal or quasi-judicial body or if allowed the aforesaid professional dress.

INSIDE THE HEARING ROOM

The Inquiry Officer should understand that he has all powers to conduct orderly, efficient and fair hearing.

- The hearings should be scheduled in such a way that the parties are prevented from spending unreasonable length of time before the chamber of the inquiry officer.

- The quasi-judicial officer should take utmost care to ensure that no prejudice or bias is perceived either by his words or by his conduct, including but not limited to bias based on race, sex, religion, caste, sex, disability, age, or socio-economical status and shall not permit his staff/officials under his control to do so.

- In order to obviate any dispute at a later state as to what happened before the Inquiry Officer during the course of inquiry, the statement of the Inquiry Officer in this regard will be generally accepted as correct [*Union of India vs. T.R.Verma*][66]. The Inquiry Officer should therefore maintain a daily order sheet recording in brief the daily happenings on the day of inquiry. The Daily Order Sheet is the property of the Inquiry Officer and other parties including the Presenting Officer, if any, do not have any right to record anything therein, except to append their signature at the end of the proceedings of the day. In the event of any difference of opinion, the aggrieved party may submit a written representation to the Inquiry Officer.

---

[66] AIR 1957 Sc. 882

- Unless there is good reason to adjourn (for instance, the defendant demonstrates his physical inability to attend the hearing on the appointed day), and if the Inquiry Officer is satisfied himself that adequate opportunities have already been offered to the defendant(s), he is expected to conduct the hearing ex-parte based on the written submissions and material evidence, if any, available on record.

- Accept written statements, if any, filed by the parties, additional evidences and testimonials and acknowledge them into the record. All evidences relied upon for the decision must be part of the record – all oral testimony, all physical exhibits presented, and third-party information collected through investigations. It is advisable to have them read before the parties, unless they are voluminous. Copies of the written statements submitted by one party may be furnished to the opponent if he desires so.

- The officer conducting quasi-judicial proceedings should refrain from making opinions and personal commentary on the matters under consideration.

- Formal rules of procedure as adopted by the traditional court system will not apply; however, fundamental due process shall be accorded. Documentary evidence may be presented in the form of a copy or the original. Upon request, parties shall be given an opportunity to compare the copy with the original.

- Witnesses need not be present in the hearing room during the hearing until such time as they are called in to testify. Witnesses may be instructed to wait outside the hearing room and can be called in one by one.

- Defendants and witnesses who wish to testify must declare that he or she will testify truthfully by taking an oath or affirmation in the following form:

'Do you swear or affirm that the evidence you are about to give will be the truth, the whole truth, and nothing but the truth?'

- Any willful false swearing on the part of any witness or person giving evidence before the Commission or Board as to any material fact in the proceedings shall be deemed to be perjury and shall be punished in the manner prescribed by law for such offence. For detailed knowledge of legal provisions relating to false evidence, readers may refer to Chapter 9.

RULES OF EVIDENCE

All evidences of a type of commonly relied upon by administrative/judicial authorities shall be admissible, irrespective of their admissibility in the Court of law. Generally, any evidence should be allowed to be presented which will be helpful and which has some reliability. Emotional and speculative presentations should be discouraged, but they never can be completely avoided. Irrelevant, immaterial, harassing, defamatory or unduly repetitive evidences may be excluded. Hearsay evidence may be used for the limited purpose of supplementing or explaining other evidences, but it shall not be *per se* sufficient to support a finding.

Thus, evidences must be relevant to the issue under consideration. It can be substantial evidence, competent evidence and material evidence. Substantial evidence is one which provides a factual basis. It refers to evidence that a reasonable mind could accept as adequate to support a conclusion. It is more than mere scintilla and of remarkable legal significance, credible and of concrete nature.

Competence Evidence is clear and convincing evidence which tends to prove the matter in dispute. For instance, production of a writing where its contents are subject of dispute or production of a weapon with which the murder was committed is competence evidence.

Documentary/material evidences may be presented in the form of a photocopy or the original and the other party/parities shall be given opportunity to compare the copy with the original document. A witness must depose not to his knowledge but also to his cause of knowledge, that is, it is not competent for a witness to depose what a third party had told him.

Justice Krishna Iyer in the case of *State Of Haryana And Anr. vs Rattan Singh*[67] wrote,

'It is well settled that in a domestic enquiry the strict and sophisticated rules of evidence under the Evidence Act may not apply. All materials which are logically probative for a prudent mind are permissible. There is no allergy to hearsay evidence provided it has reasonable nexus and creditability. It is true that departmental authorities and administrative tribunals must be careful in evaluating such material and should not glibly swallow what is strictly speaking not relevant under the Indian Evidence Act.'

Inquiry Officers are required to reduce their findings into a written order which should invariably include the nature of dispute under adjudication including the substance and source of the evidence, the findings of facts and appreciation of evidences which supports the decision, the determination of the issue and subsequent action to be taken in the light of the decision made. The record of the hearing and the findings of fact and the decision must be provided at no cost to the parties.

Burden of Proof

The allocation of the burden of proof in both civil and criminal trials turns on the decision as to who should bear the risk of losing the case. That allocation is decided by common law and by statute.

Preponderance of evidence

A preponderance of the evidence means not necessarily the larger number of witnesses, but that amount of evidence which, on the whole and when fairly and impartially considered, provides the stronger impression and is more clear and convincing when weighted against the opposing evidence.

The decision should be communicated to the parties concerned by way of an order, as soon as possible after the final hearing. The order will set out the aggrieved parties' right of appeal.

---

[67] AIR 1977 SC 1512, 1977 LablC 845, (1982) ILLJ 46 SC

CHAPTER 6
DRAFTING OF QUASI-JUDICIAL ORDERS

The entire adjudicative function, including drafting of final order, is entrusted to the quasi-judicial officer. Drafting of final orders is an essential component of quasi-judicial proceedings. It is the 'written word' which is the source of authority and delivery of justice. The time to draft an order comes when the entire hearing of the case is over. It is not enough that the decision be correct – it must also be fair, reasoned, and readily understandable. The order should reflect the decision of the authority in a clear and accurate way and it should speak for itself. It should be understandable without referring to any external material/documents. Stereotyped formats of proceedings should be avoided as they would lead to non-application of mind of the Inquiry Officer.

Though it may be imprudent to prescribe a 'definite stereotype format' for drafting of quasi-judicial, as it goes against the very principle of application of mind, the order may contain the following basic structural ingredients.

1. Introductory passage setting forth the nature of the case and identification of the parties to the issue.

2. Setting out of the facts of the case

3. The issues involved and the rules/laws that govern the issues

4. Applying the law to the facts

5. Arriving at the decision/conclusion

6. Operative portion of the order

The introductory paragraph should disclose the essence of the case; what it is about; who the parties are; and the issue involved. Chronological narration of facts and the recording of facts and evidences made during the course of inquiry will bring all the facts and details at one place. A brief discussion of the facts and issues can be made and the issues involved should be addressed to the point. If there is any disputed fact, it may either be decided during the course of discussion of the facts itself or it may be left for decision at a later state when the Inquiry Officer deals with the issues of the case. However, it should be specifically mentioned that the fact is disputed one and it will be dealt with in the forthcoming portion of the order. As regards the undisputed facts, they should be stated fairly, accurately and without any exaggeration or understatement. The authority has a liberty to interpret the law strictly or liberally according to the objective of the statute governing such laws. For instance, social security laws in India warrant liberal interpretation of the provisions. But the liberty to make liberal interpretations cannot be applied to 'facts' of the case.

Any attempt to ignore or omit the evidences, arguments, and case laws professed by the parties should be avoided. The Supreme Court in the case of *M.V. Bijlani vs Union Of India & Ors*[68] observed, '...the Enquiry Officer who performs a quasi-judicial function, who upon analysing the documents must arrive at a conclusion that there had been a preponderance of probability to prove the charges on the basis of materials on record. While doing so, he cannot take into consideration any irrelevant fact. He cannot refuse to consider the relevant facts. He cannot shift the burden of proof. He cannot reject the relevant testimony of the witnesses only on the basis of surmises and conjectures. He cannot enquire into the allegations with which the delinquent officer had not been charged with.'

.Summarizing the evidences will demonstrate to the reader that the Inquiry Officer has a better understanding of the evidences.

Legal analysis may follow the brief discussion of facts and evidences. It involves evaluation of facts vis-à-vis legal provisions. The disputes may relate to (i) facts only (ii) legal provisions only (iii) facts and legal provisions (iv) application of the legal provisions to the facts of the case. In India, the provisions of the

---

[68] (2006) 5 SCC 88

Employees' Provident Funds and Miscellaneous Provisions Act 1952 apply to any scheduled industry employing twenty or more persons. It however provides that apprentices, if any, appointed under the Apprenticeship Act of 1961 are 'excluded employees'. If an employer challenges the applicability of the Act on the premise that he engages only 15 employees and not 20, it is a question of fact. Rather, if he argues that he engages 15 employees and the other 5 are trainees, it is question of law – whether the trainees fall within the meaning of 'excluded employees'.

More complex the facts and nature of legal issues involved, more deep should be the analysis of facts and evidences. After forming a concrete opinion, the decision should be justified with reasons. The first thing to do by the Inquiry Officer is to make sure he understands the case. This means being familiar with the brief facts of the case. He should marshal the material facts, appreciate evidences, identify the applicable rules of law and relevant provisions of the statute, and determine the issue on proper application of mind. Issues which are, in the opinion of the authority, irrelevant to the case but are strongly pressed for by the parties should be discussed in the order only to the extent enough to show that they have been considered. Once the issues are identified, the authority should ascertain whether he has statutory jurisdiction to hear the case.

The decision may be communicated either orally or in writing. Where the final decision is on a point of fact or it requires to be communicated to the parties immediately, then the decision may be communicated orally. This is called *'ex tempore'* judgment. Reading of the operative portion of the order will be deemed to be pronouncement of the order. When there is no urgency involved in announcement of the decision, or when the issue involves complex matters like assessment of Income Tax, etc, the order may be reserved and a written order is given.

Though it has become very common nowadays to use meta-discourse like – *'after careful consideration, having read all the papers, on proper application of mind'* etc, it is averse to a good drafting. After completing the draft, review and revise it if necessary to make it more professional.

REQUISITES OF A JUDICIAL DECISION

The requisites of a judicial decision were laid down by the Supreme Court in *Bharat Bank Ltd, Delhi vs. Employees of Bharat Bank Ltd.*, Delhi[69]. Their Lordships quoted with approval following passage from *Cooper vs. Wilson*, 1937, 2KB 309 at page 340:—

'A true judicial decision presuppose an existing dispute between two or more parties and then four requisites: (1) The presentation (not necessarily orally) of their case by the parties to the dispute (2) If the dispute between them is a question of fact, the ascertainment of the fact by means of evidence adduced by the parties to the dispute and often with the assistance of arguments by or on behalf of the parties on the evidence (3) If the dispute between them is a question of law, the submissions on the legal arguments by the parties, and (4) A decision which disposes of the whole matter by a finding upon the facts in dispute and application of the law of the land to the facts so found, including wherever required a ruling upon any disputed question of law.'

ORDER SHOULD CONTAIN REASONS

In the case of *Union of India vs. M.L. Kapoor*[70], their Lordships of Supreme Court observed as under –

'If the statute requires recording of reasons, then it is the statutory requirement and, therefore, there is no scope for further inquiry. But even when the statute does not impose such an obligation it is necessary for the quasi-judicial authorities to record reason as it is only visible safeguard against possible injustice and arbitrariness and affords protection to the person adversely affected. Reasons are the links between the material on which certain conclusions are based and the actual conclusions. They disclose how the mind is applied to the subject-matter for a decision, whether it is purely administrative or quasi-judicial. They should reveal rational nexus between the facts considered and the

---

[69] AIR 1950 SC 188
[70] AIR 1974 SC 87

conclusion reached. Only in this way can opinions or decisions recorded be shown to be manifestly just and reasonable.'

JUDICIAL DISCIPLINE - *RATIO DECIDENDI*

Article 141 of the Constitution mandates that the law declared by the Supreme Court be binding on all courts[71] within the territory of India. The Tribunals across the country are obliged to follow the law laid down by the Supreme Court. In the case of *Jain Exports vs. Union of India*[72], the Supreme Court upheld the principle that in a tier system, decision of higher authorities are binding on lower authorities and quasi-judicial tribunals are also bound by the discipline.

It is not open to the Tribunals to say that the Supreme Court decision was not relevant simply because, it was not under the statute under which the Tribunal is working [*M.Ravji vs. State of Gujarat*[73]]

Some other terms came out of the doctrine of precedent:

Stair decisis (to stand by things decided, that is a court is bound to follow the decisions of courts higher than it, in the same hierarchy of courts within a specific jurisdiction), *Obiter dicta* (things said in passing – other legal argument or statements of principles found in judgments but not forming part of the *ratio decidendi*), *Res judicata* (a thing already adjudicated),

PRELIMINARY OBJECTIONS NEED TO BE DISPOSED FIRST

Preliminary objections on the grounds of jurisdiction, period of limitation etc may be raised by the defendants. It is imperative that such issues should be considered in the beginning of the order itself than at a later stage (Murthy, 2006). If considered necessary, such objections may be disposed of at the first instance and the officer may proceed with further only if the objections were found not sustainable.

---

[71] The Supreme Court is not bound by its own previous decision
[72] (1988) 3 SCC 579
[73] 89 STC 228, 234 (Guj.)]

CITATION OF CASE LAWS

While drafting quasi-judicial orders, the authority may have to assert some fact or point of law. Where the statutory provisions are clear and directly supporting such assertions of facts/propositions of law, then the work of the authority is lessened. Otherwise, he is burdened with an additional duty to demonstrate an authority/judicial sanction for his assertion. This is why citations of case laws are important. The law is as it is not because you say so, or a legal textbook prescribes it so, but because it has a legal sanction and the citations makes your assertions linked to recognized source of law. It is not necessary to rely on the case laws the parties cited. The quasi-judicial officer himself can do his own research to verify the authorities on which he may rely upon.

Citation of case laws should however be used judiciously. A simple matter would be made complex by elaborate citation of case laws. If the provisions of the enactment are so clear that there is no room for ambiguity, there is usually no need to refer to case laws. While citing case laws, one must distinguish between the *ratio decidendi* of the case from *obiter dicta*.

BREVITY OF ORDER

Brevity, simplicity and clarity are the hallmarks of a good quasi-judicial order. Brevity promotes clarity of the order. Judicial writing should be simple and direct.

It is said, Winston Churchill, soon after his becoming the First Lord of the Admiralty in 1939 sent a memo to every admiral of the British Fleet, 'Pray Sir, tell me on one side of one sheet of paper, how the Royal Navy is preparing for the modern warfare.' Churchill would have been precautious as he would have received a 400-pages voluminous report from the admirals otherwise.

While brevity and simplicity are desirable qualities of a quasi-judicial order, it should not be done at the cost of fairness, openness and detailed reasoning of the order.

In the case of *B. Vishwanath vs. State of Karnataka*[74] the Supreme Court observed,

'Coming to the facts of the case, the only thing that needs to be observed is that the impugned judgment and order of the High Court has one characteristic, i.e., brevity. It has no other characteristic. It does not even refer to the various aspects and briefly refers to the evidence of the witnesses. It needs no emphasis that the Appellate Court exercising appellate powers has not only to consider various points but objectively and critically analyse the evidence.'

The authority should bear in mind that pleadings are no evidence and a thorough reading of all documents filed during the course of hearing and a discussion of them are essential in order to arrive at the right conclusion.

STYLE OF WRITING

Bombastic or flowery words and expressions should be avoided. They should be succinct and lucid statements of facts and law, coherent in logic, to bring out the truth, and no material fact should be omitted. While it is always good to make the writing lively and elegant to interest the reader, it should not however require him to have a dictionary at hand while reading the order.

Professor Bernard Witkin argues that judges should avoid such 'even if' or 'assuming arguendo that' rulings [See B.E.Witkin, Manual on Appellate Court Opinions§ 81 (1977)]. Statements such as 'even if the facts were otherwise', or 'assuming arguendo that we had not concluded thus and so' undermine the authority of the order.

Have a relook before the order is finalized, to see that all the issues have been addressed, all the facts significant to the decision have been specified, review the legal issues and ensure that the decision follows from the facts enumerated and discussion made.

---

[74] 2008 CriLJ 1947, JT 2008(2) SC305, 2008(3) KarLJ 299, 2008(2) SCALE 353, (2008)11SCC168

Taking serious note of the fact that a quasi-judicial order was drafted by the subordinate officials in the Central Board of Excise and Customs, the Tribunal came heavily on the CBEC, observing that –

A quasi-judicial officer has to apply his own mind to the facts and circumstances of the case and reach at his own decision unfettered by anything else. From that it follows that even the narration of facts in an adjudication order has to be drafted by the adjudicating officer himself.

APPLICATION OF MIND

Application of mind is a prerequisite in deciding cases. If an order is written without application of mind, legal mistakes or factual errors are bound to occur.

In the case of *Hira Sugar Employees Co-operative Consumers Stores Limited v P.P. Korvekar*[75], the Karnataka High Court observed,

'Application of mind cannot be inferred unless mind is disclosed by the authority passing the order, and disclosure of mind is best done by recording reasons for the conclusion being arrived at. An order passed without proper application of mind by the authority must be deemed to be per se arbitrary and even malafide in law, even when the authority passing the same may in fact have no malice against the party who suffers such an order. The duty cast upon a statutory judicial or quasi-judicial authority to act only upon proper application of mind, fairly and objectively and to record reasons in support, of the order made whether the same be interim or final, can hardly be under played let alone undermined. This so particularly where the order passed by the authority creates or fastens liabilities against a citizen, for one of the most valued guarantees which the system provides to the citizen is a fair, objective, non-

---

[75] 1995 (70) FLR 914, ILR 1995 KAR 127

discriminatory, treatment to his rights free from the vice of arbitrariness.'

OPERATIVE PORTION OF THE ORDER

The enforcement of order is based on the operative portion of the order. Hence, the authority should bear in mind that the directions given to the parties must be clear, unambiguous and executable. Ambiguity in the operative portion of the order not only causes inconvenience to the parties but also creates a dead lock in resolving the dispute (Murthy, 2006). All orders and/or directions of the authority shall be stated in clear and precise terms in the last paragraph of the order. The time-limit if any for compliance of the directions/order may also be clearly stated in the order and whether the time stipulated should be reckoned from the date of order or date of receipt of the order by the parties. It is always advisable to fix the time-frame for compliance of the order from the date of receipt of the order by the parties concerned. The authority who issues the order should initial corrections, if any, and affix his signature at the bottom of each page.

CHAPTER 7
JUDICIAL REVIEW OF QUASI-JUDICIAL DECISIONS

The power of judicial review of the High Courts under Article 226 and 227 and that of the Supreme Court under Article 32 and 136 is a constitutional guarantee and cannot be taken away by parliamentary enactments. If the quasi-judicial bodies act without jurisdiction or fails to exercise their jurisdiction, or when the orders passed by them are arbitrary, perverse or *malafide*, or if they have not followed the principles of natural justice, or their orders are *ultra-vires* of the parent Act or the Constitution, or grave injustice is perpetuated by their orders[76], or if the order is such that no reasonable man would have made it[77], such orders can be set aside by the High Court or by the Supreme Court. (Bilal, 2004)

The judiciary can intervene in the administrative/quasi-judicial acts under the following circumstances.

LACK OF JURISDICTION

Lack of Jurisdiction, that is, when the administrator acts without authority or beyond the scope of his authority or outside the geographical jurisdiction of his authority. It is technically called *'overfeasance'* (excess of authority). When a judicial/quasi-judicial authority exceeds his jurisdiction, the subject matter with regard to which he had exercised such excess of jurisdiction is said to be *'coram non judice'* (before one who is not the judge) and hence become void. Those orders which the quasi-judicial authority has no power to make under the enabling statutory provisions are subject to judicial nullification under this category.

- Patent and latent want of jurisdiction – *defectus jurisdictionis* and *defectus triationis*.

---

[76] Dhanalakshmi Cotton Mills Ltd vs. CTR, AIR 1995 SC,
[77] CIT vs. Radha Kishan, AIR 1975, SC 893

Lack of competency in a Court may arise in one of the following two ways:

(i) A court may lack jurisdiction over the cause or matter or over the parties.

(ii) It may also lack competence because of failure to comply with such procedural requirements as are necessary for the exercise of power by the Court.

Both are jurisdictional defects. The first mentioned of these is commonly known in the law as a *'patent'* or 'total' want of jurisdiction or a *defectus jurisdictionis*. The second one – a 'latent' or 'contingent' want of jurisdiction or a *defectus triationis*. Both classes of jurisdictional defect result in judgments or orders which are void.

It is however well established that a petitioner can hardly succeed on the ground against the jurisdiction of the authority, whose order he is challenging unless he has taken the ground before the authority making the order. Such failure amounts to absence of diligence on the part of the petitioner. The High Court of Kerala in the case of *Mairyan vs. State of Kerala*[78] observed as follows:

'The principle is that the High Court refuses to exercise its jurisdiction in favour of a writ applicant who sat on the fence, took the chance of the decision before that authority and then turned round and challenged the jurisdiction of the authority.'

Thus a latent lack of jurisdiction can itself arise when the lack of jurisdiction has to be spelt out on the basis of certain facts which may or may not be known to the Writ petitioner. If he knew the facts at the time he took the chance of the decision before the Tribunal and did not disclose those facts and did not raise the point of jurisdiction before the Tribunal but took it for the first time in proceedings under Article 226 of the Constitution, the high courts, in exercise of their discretionary power, can usually decline jurisdiction. But if on the other hand, the lack of jurisdiction is not

---

[78] 1965 Ker LT

latent in that manner but was patent, the fact that he knew about the lack of jurisdiction when he took the chance of the decision before the Quasi-judicial Tribunal does not matter and the High Court ought to interfere.

ERROR OF LAW

Error of Law, occurs when the quasi-judicial officer misinterprets the law and thus imposes upon the citizen, obligations which are not required by the content of law. It is an improper way of doing something or an improper performance of a legal duty. It is technically called *'misfeasance.'*

ERROR IN FACT FINDING

Error in Fact Finding takes place when the quasi-judicial officer makes a mistake in the discovery of facts and acts on wrong presumptions. As a general rule, higher courts used to review questions of law and not questions of fact. Dickinson's conclusion is useful here: 'When the courts are unwilling to review, they are tempted to explain by the easy device of calling the question one of "fact"; and when otherwise disposed, they say that is a question of "law".'

It has been pointed out by many judicial pronouncements that the findings could be said to be perverse only if it is shown that such a finding is not supported by any evidence or is entirely opposed to the whole body of evidence adduced [*Doom Dooma Tea Company Ltd vs. Assam Chah Karmachari Sangha and another*[79]]. Merely that the authority could possibly come to a different view on the evidence recorded would not make the finding of the domestic tribunal perverse. A wrong finding is not necessarily a perverse finding. A perverse finding is not only against the weight of the evidence, but is altogether against the evidence itself. Again, a finding cannot be held perverse more because it is possible for another authority on the materials to come to a different finding.

---

[79] (1960) II LLJ 56 SC

Thus, while a finding based on no evidence constitutes an error of law, an error in appreciation of evidence or in drawing inferences does not constitute an error of law, except where it is perverse, that is to say, such a conclusion as no person properly instructed in law would have reached, or it is based on evidence which is legally inadmissible [*Board of Wakfs vs. Hadi* [80]].

On the other hand, if the evidence is supported by evidence on record, no interference is called for even though the court considers that another view is possible [*Maharastra S.B.S.E vs.Gandhi* [81]].

The following has been usually held to be an error of fact:

- a 'wrong' finding of fact; a 'perverse' finding of fact; a finding of fact 'contrary to the overwhelming weight of the evidence'; a finding of fact 'against the evidence and the weight of the evidence'; a finding of fact that 'ignores the probative force of the evidence which is all one way' and a finding of fact that 'no reasonable person could have made.'

ABUSE OF AUTHORITY

Abuse of authority is said to have made when the quasi-judicial officer uses his authority (or power or discretion) vindictively to harm some person – by actually doing, to the prejudice of another, something one ought not to do. It is technically called *'malfeasance.'*

Colourable exercise of Power:

The phrase 'colourable exercise of power' is used by Courts to denounce an abuse of power by the lower courts. Power is granted to an authority on the *bona fide* belief that it must be used honestly and only for the purpose which it is granted. The power available to the authorities should be exercised though in the facts and circumstances of an individual case, it may be inexpedient to exercise such power or the exercise of such power may stand vitiated if it is shown to have been exercised in a

---

[80] (1993)Supp 1 SCC 192: AIR 1992 SC 1083
[81] (1991) 2 SCC 716

manner which may be called colourable exercise of power or an abuse of power, what at times is also termed in administrative law as 'fraud on power.'[*S.S.Shekhavat vs. Union of India & Ors,*][82]. In *Somawanti vs. State of Punjab*[83] the Supreme Court held that the power must be exercised for the purpose for which it was conferred and if it was used for different purpose, there was colourable exercise of power and the order will be a nullity.

ERROR OF PROCEDURE

'Due process' is the basis of governmental action in a democracy. Quasi-judicial authorities have to act according to certain procedures laid down by law, and if they fail to follow the prescribed procedure, the courts have a right to question the legality of their actions. *Error of Procedure takes place* when the quasi-judicial officer does not follow the laid down procedure, the order will get struck down by the Court. However, the substance of the error should have been so serious that the parties have been prejudiced thereby. Examples are denial of sufficient opportunities to the parties to defend their case, or failure to comply with the rules and regulations which results in violation of natural justice in some way, etc.

ERROR APPARENT ON THE FACE OF THE ORDER

If there is an error of law, which is apparent on the face of the record, a decision of an inferior court or a tribunal may be quashed by a *writ of certiorari*. But an error of fact, 'however grave it may appear to be' cannot be corrected by a writ of certiorari. Where two views are possible, if an inferior court or tribunal takes one view, it cannot be corrected by the higher courts.

A Sri Lankan court explained, 'What is contemplated by ''manifest error'' is no more than error which must be plain on the face of the admissible record, not error which can be discovered only after assiduous search beyond its face.' Errors apparent on the

---

[82] W.P.(C) No. 2003/2006 Del.HC

[83] AIR 1963 SC 151;(1963)2 SCR 774

face of the proceedings are always treated as errors of jurisdiction for the purpose of quashing by issuing a writ of certiorari. It should be noted that the error which is apparent should not be mere accidental or formal error which would always be set right by amendment. It must be a substantial error and one which goes to the roof of the matter.

NON-APPLICATION OF MIND

If a discretionary power granted to a quasi-judicial authority by a statute is exercised in a mechanical way, without proper application of mind to the facts and circumstances, the authority is deemed not to have exercised its discretion at all. Abdication of functions, acting under the dictation of the administrative superiors etc also fetters on the exercise of discretion, and therefore makes the order susceptible to judicial invalidation on the grounds of non-application of mind. If the accused/defendant can demonstrate that the order suffers from non-application of mind, the same may be called in question before a competent court of law [*Ramesh Lal Jain vs.Naginder Singh Rana,*[84]]

WRIT JURISDICTION OF HIGH COURTS/SUPREME COURT

Persons who are affected by one or more of the aforesaid cases can seek the intervention of judiciary for remedy (Laxmikanth, 2002).

The quasi-judicial orders are always subject to the supervisory/appellate jurisdiction of the High Courts and Supreme Court under Articles 32, 136, 226 and 227 of the Indian Constitution. *Certiorari* and *prohibition* lie only in respect of judicial or quasi-judicial acts[85]. The principle *audi alteram partem* also applies only to judicial or quasi- judicial proceedings.

Article 226

---

[84] (2006) 1 SCC 294
[85] Halsbury's Laws of England, 3rd Edn. Vol. 11, p. 55, para. 114

Article 32 of the Indian Constitution empowers the Supreme Court to issue writs for the enforcement of the Fundamental Rights of citizens guaranteed to them under Article 14 to 31 of the Constitution. Article 226 empowers the High Courts to issue the Writs not only for the enforcement of the fundamental rights but also for other purposes. Thus the writ jurisdiction of high courts is wider than that of the Supreme Court.

Article 227

Article 227 of the Indian Constitution derives its origin from Section 15 of the Indian High Courts Act, 1861, Section 107 of the Government of India Act, 1915-1919, Section 224 of the Government of India Act, 1935 which conferred upon each of the Chartered High Courts the power of superintendence over all the subordinate courts subject to its appellate jurisdiction.

DIFFERENCE BETWEEN ARTICLE 226 AND 227

Both Articles 226 and 227 of the Constitution, in substance, provide for the same relief, viz., scrutiny of records and control of subordinate courts and tribunals and, therefore, the exercise of jurisdiction under these Articles would fall within the expression 'Revisional Jurisdiction' or 'Power of Superintendence.'

Under Article 226, the High Courts have power to issue directions, orders and Writs to any person or authority including any Government. Under Article 227 every High Court has the power of superintendence over all courts and tribunals throughout its jurisdictional territory. The power to issue writ is not the same as the power of superintendence. By no stretch of imagination can a writ in the nature of *Habeas Corpus* or *Mandamus* or *quo warranto* or prohibition or *certiorari* be equated with the power of superintendence. These are writs directed against persons, authorities and the State. The power of superintendence conferred upon every High Court by Article 227 is a supervisory jurisdiction intended to ensure that subordinate courts and tribunals act within the limits of their authority and according to law [*State of Gujarat v. Vakhatsinghji Vajesinghji Vaghela*[86]. The orders, directions and Writs under Article 226 is mainly for remedial measures and are not intended for the power of supervision over lower courts/tribunals.

The jurisdiction of the High Court under Article 226 of the Constitution is limited to seeing that the judicial or quasi-judicial tribunals or administrative bodies exercising quasi-judicial powers do not exceed their statutory jurisdiction and correctly administer the law laid down by the statute under which they act. So long as the hierarchy of officers and appellate authorities created by a statute function within their ambit, the manner in which they do so can be no ground for interference.

The powers of judicial supervision of the High Court under Article 227 of the Constitution are not greater than those under Article 226 and must be limited to seeing that the tribunal functions within the limits of its authority. Under Article 226, the power of interference may extend to quashing an impugned order on the ground of a mistake apparent on the face of the record. But under Article 227 of the Constitution, the power of interference is limited to seeing that the tribunal functions within the limits of its authority.

---

[86] A.I.R. 1968 S.C. 1487, 1488

Article 226	Article 227
Normally exercised where a party is affected	Can be exercised *suo moto* (without any complaint) by the High Court as a custodian of justice
Power under Art.226 is exercised in favour of citizens for vindication of their fundamental rights/statutory rights.	Exercised by the High Court for vindication of its position as the highest judicial authority in the State
Can be claimed as a matter of right when the rights of the citizens are affected.	Cannot be claimed as a matter of right; it is totally discretionary power of the High Court.
From an order of a Single Judge passed under Article 226, a Letters Patent Appeal or an intra Court Appeal is maintainable.	No such appeal is maintainable from an order passed by a Single Judge of a High Court in exercise of power under Article227.
In almost all High Courts, rules have been framed for regulating the exercise of jurisdiction under Article 226	No such rule appears to have been framed for exercise of High Court's power under Article 227 possibly to keep such exercise entirely in the domain of the discretion of High Court.

Shalini Shyam Shetty & Another vs. Rajendra Shankar Patil reported in 2010 (3) KLT 86 (SN) (C.No.90)

Note: The High Court's power under Article 227 of the Constitution though initially shown to be restricted only to the case of grave dereliction of duties and gross violation, to be used/exercised most sparingly in cases of grave injustice, but there is a shift of the paradigm. The trend is now liberalized. It, however, cannot be used as an appellate or revisional power. The High Court in exercise of its power will not substitute its own judgment to that of an inferior Court on a question of fact or interfere with the legitimate exercise of powers/jurisdiction by the inferior Court, unless it is arbitrary, capricious or there is error of finding of jurisdictional fact [*Achutananda Baidya vs Prafullya Kumar Gayen And Others*,][87]

Two kinds of Writs under the extraordinary constitutional provisions of Article 32 and 226 are usually issued against quasi-judicial authorities. They are: *Writ of Certiorari* and *Writ of Prohibition*. They are meant to confine the quasi-judicial authorities within the confines of their legal jurisdiction. The grounds on which the two Writs are issued are almost similar, but there are material differences in the scope of these two Writs.

WRIT OF PROHIBITION

It literally means 'to forbid.' It is issued by a higher court to a lower court when the latter exceeds its jurisdiction. It can be issued only against judicial and quasi-judicial authorities and not against administrative authorities. Hence, its importance as a tool of judicial control over administration is highly restricted.

A writ of prohibition can be issued only when three conditions are satisfied, namely, 1) that the authority against whom it is sought is about to exercise judicial or quasi-judicial power, 2) that the exercise of such power is unauthorized by law and 3) that it will result in injury for which no other adequate remedy exists. It is provided for an extraordinary remedy and can be issued only in cases of extreme necessity. Before such writ is issued, the Court must arrive at a finding that the party aggrieved had applied in vain to the inferior Tribunal for relief. It is also trite that a writ of prohibition is not to be claimed as a matter of right but the same is granted to do justice and the same must be based on sound judicial discretion depending upon the facts and circumstances of each case. In *U.P.Sales Tax Service Association vs. Taxation Bar Association*, the Apex Court observed that a writ or order of

---

[87] AIR 1997 SC 2077, 1997 (2) CTC 333, JT 1997 (5) SC 75

prohibition cannot be issued prohibiting a quasi-judicial or statutory authority from discharging its statutory functions or transferring those functions to another jurisdiction. Exercise of such power, the Supreme Court held, generates its rippling effect on the subordinate judiciary and statutory functionaries [*Allauddin Charities And Zakath vs Hameed Ali And Ors.*][88] In *Guduthur Bros vs. The Income Tax Officer*[89], the apex court refused to issue a writ of prohibition when merely a show cause notice was issued. A writ of prohibition is a negative remedy.

WRIT OF CERTIORARI

It literally means 'to be certified'. It is issued by a higher court to a lower court (including the quasi-judicial agencies) for transferring the records of proceedings of a case pending with the latter, for the purpose of determining the legality of its proceedings or for giving fully and a more satisfactory effect to them than could be done in the lower court. Thus, unlike the Prohibition, which is only preventive, the Certiorari is both preventive as well as curative. Like Prohibition, it can be issued only against judicial and quasi-judicial authorities and not against administrative authorities.

They are issued at different stages of the proceedings. If a quasi-judicial authority, having no jurisdiction in a matter, takes it up for hearing, the aggrieved person can pray for issue of Prohibition. If the said quasi-judiciary authority had already heard the matter and given his decision, the proper remedy to the situation lies in Writ of Certiorari and not Prohibition. Certiorari quashes the decision on the grounds of excess or want of jurisdiction. Prohibition issues where the quasi-judicial authority has not reached and passed the stage of giving his decision. Prohibition lies where the matter is still pending and there is some scope for prevention.

---

[88] 2002 (1) ALD 67, 2002 (2) ALT 534
[89] 1960 AIR 1326

Article 136

The powers of the Supreme Court under Article 136 are very wide, residuary and special in nature. To meet the ends of justice in exceptional circumstances, when all other ordinary recourses to justice fail, the Apex Court may step in the interest of safeguarding justice by allowing a Special Leave Petition (SLP) under Article 136. Article 136(1) of the Constitution confers power on the Supreme Court to grant special leave to appeal from any judgment, decree, or order in any cause or matter passed by any Court or Tribunal[90] in the territory of India.

Article 136(1) uses the term 'tribunal' to contradistinguish it from a traditional 'court' and the term '*tribunal*' takes into its purview all quasi-judicial bodies. The Supreme Court has held that any authority, which is empowered by statutory provisions, 'to exercise any adjudicating power of the State', would be held to be a 'tribunal'.

In *Management of Wegner and Co vs. Their Workmen*[91], the Supreme Court held that in entertaining appeals under Article 136 from Industrial Tribunals, the Supreme Court does not act as a regular court of appeal on facts but decides the general question of law to guide industrial adjudication. Thus, the questions of facts decided by the quasi-judicial forums are not reviewed by the Supreme Court unless the decision of the authority is patently perverse and manifestly unjust. It would intervene in terms of Article 136 only when there is a gross violation of principles of natural justice causing grave and substantial injustice, or there is an important question of law raised, or there is any special or extraordinary circumstances warranting the intervention of the Supreme Court.

The scope of the jurisdiction of the Supreme Court in dealing with Writ Petitions under Article 32 was examined by a Special Bench of the Supreme Court in *Smt Ujjam Bai vs State of Uttar Pradesh*[92]. The decision would show that it is common

---

[90] Other than those constituted under any law relating to armed forces
[91] AIR 1964 SC 864
[92] 1962 AIR 1621, 1963 SCR (1) 778

ground before the Court that in three classes of cases, a question of the enforcement of the fundamental rights may arise:

(i) Where action taken under a statute is *ultra vires* of the Constitutional provisions

(ii) Where the statute is *intra vires*, but the action taken is without jurisdiction, and

(iii) Where the action taken is procedurally *ultra vires* as where a quasi-judicial authority under an obligation to act judicially passes an order in violation of the principles of natural justice.

DEPARTMENTAL INQUIRY VIS-À-VIS CRIMINAL PROCEEDINGS

Departmental inquiry is a quasi-judicial proceeding, and is different from a criminal proceeding. The scope of a criminal trial is to determine whether an offence against the law of the land has been committed, and if so, to punish the person if he is found guilty of the offence. The scope of departmental inquiry is to determine whether a public servant has committed a misconduct or delinquency and if so, whether he deserves to be retained in service or reverted or reduced in rank or otherwise suitably dealt with for his delinquency or misconduct.

In a criminal trial, the prosecution will have to prove its case beyond all reasonable doubt. In a disciplinary proceeding, the decision is taken based on preponderance of probability.

Evidence Act does not apply to a disciplinary proceeding. Material which is not strictly admissible in evidence in a court of law can nevertheless be admitted into evidence in a departmental inquiry and relied upon, provided the Inquiry Officer is satisfied about the credibility of the evidence so admitted. Where there is 'some' evidence, which the Disciplinary Authority had accepted, and that evidence may reasonably support the conclusion that the delinquent is guilty of the charge, the decision based on such evidence cannot be questioned before a court of law. High court has no power to re-appreciate evidence of a departmental inquiry to which technical rules of evidence do not apply [*State of Orissa vs. Murlidhar Jena*[93]].

In *Workmen of Balmadies Estates vs. Management of Balmadies Estates*[94] , the Apex Court again held as under: '... The assessment of evidence in a domestic enquiry is not required to be made by applying the same yardstick as a civil court could do when a *lis* is brought before it. The Evidence Act, 1872 is not applicable to the proceeding in a domestic enquiry so far as the domestic enquiries are concerned, though the principles of fairness are to apply. It is also fairly well settled that in a domestic enquiry guilty may not be established beyond reasonable doubt and the proof of misconduct would be sufficient. In a domestic enquiry all materials which are logically probative including hearsay evidence can be acted upon provided it has a reasonable nexus and credibility.'

Hearsay evidence which is not admissible in a criminal proceeding may be accepted in a departmental inquiry provided it has reasonable nexus and credibility. To what extent such evidence may be received and relied upon must depend on the facts and circumstances of each case, and the Inquiry Officer must be careful in evaluating such material.

The Supreme Court held in the case of *State of Andhra Pradesh vs. S. Sree Ramarao*[95] that the rule followed in a criminal trial that an offence is not established unless proved beyond reasonable doubt does not apply to departmental inquiries.

In *Usha Breco Mazdoor Sangh vs. Management of Usha Breco Ltd.*[96], the Apex Court has observed as under:

'In a departmental proceeding, standard of proof is not that misconduct must be proved beyond all reasonable doubt but standard of proof is as to whether the test of preponderance of probability has been met. ...'

---

[93] AIR (1963) SC 404
[94] (2008) 4 SCC 517
[95] AIR 1963 SC 1723
[96] (2008) 5 SCC 554

Likewise, in *Noida Entrepreneurs Association vs. Noida & Ors.*[97], the Apex Court held that 'the standard of proof required in the departmental proceeding is not the same as required to prove a criminal charge and even if there is an acquittal in the criminal proceedings the same does not bar departmental proceedings...'.

Similarly, in *Manager, Reserve Bank of India, Bangalore vs. S. Mani & ors.*[98] , the Apex Court considered the effect of acquittal in a criminal case and held that merely acquittal of an employee in a criminal case would not entitle him for reinstatement.

---

[97] (2007) 10 SCC 385
[98] 2005 II LLJ 258

CHAPTER 8
Powers of the Inquiry Officers under the Code of Civil Procedure, 1908

The officers empowered to conduct an inquiry under the various statutes in India have been commonly vested with the powers of a civil court under the Code of Civil Procedure, 1908 for certain purposes. For instance, Section 18 of the Payment of Wages Act, 1936, Section 245U of the Income Tax Act, 1961, Section 28L of the Customs Act, 1962, Section 7 of the Equal Remuneration Act, 1976, Section 4A of the Forward Contracts (Regulation) Act, 1952, Section 24 of the Mines Act, 1952, to name a few, cast such powers of a civil court on the Inquiry Officers established under the respective statues. Similarly, many statutory Commissions/Regulatory Authorities/ Administrative Tribunals are also required to perform quasi-judicial functions. Examples are the Central Information Commission, State Information Commissions (under the Right to Information Act 2005), Telecom Regulatory Authority of India (under the Telecom Regulatory Authority of India Act 1997), Cyber Regulations Appellate Tribunal (under the Information Technology Act 2005, Insurance Regulatory and Development Authority (under the Insurance Regulatory and Development Authority Act 1999), Central Electricity Regulatory Commission (under the Electricity Regulatory Commissions Act 1998) etc.

Even the procedure for impeachment of President of India under Article 61 of the Indian Constitution is quasi-judicial. Thus, it becomes imperative for the Inquiry Officers purporting to conduct quasi-judicial proceedings to get themselves acquainted with the procedures and powers provided under the relevant provisions of the Code of Civil Procedure, 1908 for the purpose of taking evidence and of enforcing the attendance of witnesses, compelling production of documents etc in an effective manner.

Before proceeding further in to the contents of the Civil Procedure Code, it is desirable to understand the basic difference between the various terminologies – article, section and rules of orders. Though all of them are basically used for the purpose of *'numbering'*, the context of usage is different. The term 'articles' is commonly used in an fundamentally important document like an International Convention or a Constitution, 'Section' is used in the substantial laws, and 'Rules of Orders' is procedural law.

The following Sections and Rules of Orders are very relevant for conducting a quasi-judicial proceeding in India.

Relevant Sections of Civil Procedure Code (CPC)

The quasi-judicial authorities should get acquainted with the sound principles of Civil Procedure Code as well as Criminal Procedure Code and also with Indian Penal Code and the Indian Evidence Act. Keeping this in mind the relevant provisions of CPC, Cr PC and IPC and the Indian Evidence Act are included here to equip the quasi-judiciary functionaries with a strong foundation.

Section 27, 28, 30, 31 and 32

Order V, IX, XI, XIII, XVI, XVII, XVIII, XIX and XXVI

Now let us see briefly the contents of the afore-mentioned Sections and Orders.

ISSUE OF SUMMONS[99]

This topic can be divided into two parts, viz., (i) Summons to Defendants and (ii) Summons to witnesses.

Section 27: Summons to Defendants:

Where a suit has been duly instituted, a summons may be issued to the defendant to appear and answer the claim and may be served in manner prescribed *[on such day not beyond thirty days from date of the institution of the suit][100].

---

[99] Grammatically, summons is singular and its plural form is summonses
[100] Added by Act No. 46 of 1999, section 3 (*with effect from* 1-7-2002)

Section 28: Service of summons where defendant resides in another State

(1) A summons may be sent for service in another State to such Court and in such manner as may be prescribed by rules in force in that State

(2) The Court to which such summons is sent shall, upon receipt thereof, proceed as if it had been issued by such Court and shall then return the summons to the Court of issue together with the record (if any) of its proceedings with regard thereto.

(3) Where the language of the summons sent for service in another State is different from the language of the record referred to in sub-section (2), a translation of the record –

  (a) in Hindi, where the language of the Court issuing the summons is Hindi, or

  (b) in Hindi or English where the language of such record is other than Hindi or English, shall also be sent together with the record sent under that sub-section][101].

Section 30: Power to Order Discovery and The Like

Subject to such conditions and limitations as may be prescribed, the Court may, at any time, either of its own motion or on the application of any party --

(a) make such orders as may be necessary or reasonable in all matters relating to the delivery and answering of interrogatories, the admission of documents and facts, and the discovery, inspection, production, impounding and return of documents or other material objects producible as evidence;

---

[101] *Ins. by Act No. 104 of 1976, sec. 12 (*with effect from* 1-5-1977).

(b) issue summonses to persons whose attendance is required either to give evidence or to produce documents or such other objects as aforesaid;

(c) order any fact to be proved by affidavit.

Section 31: Summons to Witness

The provisions in sections 27, 28 and 29 shall apply to summonses to give evidence or to produce documents or other material objects.

Section 32: Penalty for default

The Court may compel the attendance of any person to whom a summons has been issued under section 30 and for that purpose may-

(a) issue a warrant for his arrest;

(b) attach and sell his property;

(c) impose a fine upon him *[not exceeding five thousand rupees][102];

(d) order him to furnish security for his appearance and in default commit him to the civil prison[103].

ORDER V: ISSUE AND SERVICE OF SUMMONS

Rule 9: Delivery or transmission of summons for service:-

(1) Where the defendant resides within the jurisdiction of the Court in which the suit is instituted, or has an agent resident within that jurisdiction who is empowered to accept the service of the summons, the summons shall, unless the Court otherwise directs, be delivered or sent to the proper officer to be served by him or one of his subordinates.

---

[102] *Substituted by Act No. 46 of 1999, section 4 (*with effect from* 1 -7-2002) for 'not exceeding five hundred rupees'.
[103] Generally Criminal Prison is where a convict in a criminal offence undergoes his punishment. Civil Prison is where a defaulter so declared in a civil case (like non-payment of Provident Fund dues) is kept.

(2) The proper officer may be an officer of a Court other than that in which the suit is instituted, and, where he is such an officer, the summons may be sent to him by· post or in such other manner as the Court may direct.

Rule 10 Mode of Service:-

Service of the summons shall be made by delivering or tendering a copy thereof signed by the Judge or such officer as he appoints in this behalf, and sealed with the seal of the Court.

Rule 11 Service on several defendants

Save as otherwise prescribed, where there are more defendants than one, service of the summons shall be made on each defendant.

Rule 12 Service to be on defendant in person when practicable, or on his agent:-

Wherever it is practicable service shall be made on the defendant in person, unless he has an agent empowered to accept service, in which case service on such agent shall be sufficient.

Rule 13 Service on agent by whom defendant carries on business:-

(1) In a suit relating to any business or work against a person who does not reside within the local limits of the jurisdiction of the Court from which the summons is issued, service on any manager or agent, who, at the time of service, personally carries on such business or work for such person within such limits, shall be deemed good service.

(2) For the purpose of this rule the master of a ship shall be deemed to be the agent of the owner or chartered.

Rule 15 Where service may be on an adult member of defendant's family

Where in a suit the defendant is absent from his residence at the time when the service of summons is sought to be effected on his at his residence and there is no likelihood of his being found at the residence within a reasonable time and he has no agent empowered to accept service of the summons on his behalf service may be made on any adult member of the family, whether male or female, who is residing with him.[104]

Rule 16 Person served to sign acknowledgement

Where the serving officer delivers or tenders a copy of the summons to the defendant personally, or to an agent or other person on his behalf, he shall require the signature of the person to whom the copy is so delivered or tendered to an acknowledgement of service endorsed on the original summons.

Rule 17 Procedure when defendant refuses to accept service, or cannot be found

Where the defendant or his agent or such other person as aforesaid refuses to sign the acknowledgement, or where the serving officer, after using all due and reasonable diligence, cannot find the defendant, [who is absent from his residence at the time when service is sought to be effected on him at his residence and there is no likelihood of his being found at the residence within a reasonable time] and there is no agent empowered to accept service of the summons on his behalf, nor any other person on whom service can be made, the serving officer shall affix a copy of the summons on the outer door or some other conspicuous part of the house in which the defendant ordinarily resides or carries on business or personally works for gain, and shall then return the original to the Court from which it was issued, with a report endorsed thereon or annexed thereto stating that he has so affixed the copy, the circumstances under which he did do, and the name and address of the person (if any) by whom the house was identified and in whose presence the copy was affixed.

Rule 18 Endorsement of time and manner of service

The serving officer shall, in all cases in which the summons has been served under rule 16, endorse or annex, or

---

[104] Explanation.- A servant is not a member of the family within the meaning of this rule.

cause to be endorsed or annexed, on or to the original summons, a return stating the time when and the manner in which the summons was served, and the name and address of the person (if any) identifying the person served and witnessing the delivery or tender of the summons.

Rule 19 Examination of Serving Officer

Where a summons is returned under rule 17, the Court shall, if the return under that rule has not been verified by the affidavit of the serving officer, and may, if it has been so verified, examine the serving officer on oath, or cause him to be so examined by another Court, touching his proceedings, and may make such further enquiry in the matter as it thinks fit; and shall either declare that the summons has been duly served or order such service as it thinks fit.

Rule 19-A Simultaneous issue of summons for service by post in addition to personal service

(1) The Court shall, in addition to, and simultaneously with, the issue of summons for service in the manner provided in rules 9 to 19 (both inclusive), also direct the summons to be served by registered post, acknowledgement due, addressed to the defendant, or his agent empowered to accept the service, at the place where the defendant, or his agent, actually and voluntarily resides or carries on business or personally works for gain:

Provided that nothing in this sub-rule shall require the Court to issue a summons for service by registered post, where, in the circumstances of the case, the Court considers it unnecessary.

(2) When an acknowledgement purporting to be signed by the defendant or his agent is received by the Court or the postal article containing the summons is received back by the Court with an endorsement purporting to have been made by a postal employee to the effect that the defendant or his agent had refused to take delivery of the postal article containing the summons, when tendered to him, the

Court issuing the summons shall declare that the summons had been duly served on the defendant :

Provided that where the summons was properly addressed, prepaid and duly sent by registered post, acknowledgement due, the declaration referred to in this sub-rule shall be made notwithstanding the fact that the acknowledgement having lost or mislaid, or for other reason, has been received by the Court within thirty days from the date of the issue of the summons].

Rule 20 Substituted service

(1) Where the Court is satisfied that there is reason to believe that the defendant is keeping out of the way for the purpose of avoiding service, or that for any other reason the summons cannot be served in the ordinary way, the Court shall order the summons to be served by affixing a copy thereof in some conspicuous place in the Court-house, and also upon some conspicuous part of the house (if any) in which the defendant is known to have last resided or carried on business or personally worked for gain, or in such other manner as the Court thinks fit.

[(1A) Where the Court acting under sub-rule (1) orders service by an advertisement in a newspaper, the newspaper shall be a daily newspaper circulating in the locality in which the defendant is last known to have actually and voluntarily resided, carried on business or personally worked for gain.]

(2) Effect of substituted service – service substituted by order of the Court shall be as effectual as if it had been made on the defendant personally.

(3) Where service substituted, time for appearance to be fixed – Where service is substituted by order of the Court, the Court shall fix such time for the appearance of the defendant as the case may require.

Rule 21 Service of Summons where defendant resides within the jurisdiction of another Court

A summons may be sent by the court by which it is issued, whether within or without the State, either by one of its officers or by post or by such courier service as may be approved by the High Court, by fax message or by electronic mail service or by any other means as may be provided by the rules made by the High Court to any court (not being the High Court) having jurisdiction in the place where the defendant resides.

Rule 22 Service within presidency-towns of summons issued by Courts outside

Where a summons issued by any court established beyond the limits of the towns of Calcutta, Madras and Bombay is to be served within any such limits, it shall be sent to the court of small causes within whose jurisdiction it is to be served.

Rule 23 Duty of Court to which summons is sent

The Court to which a summons is sent under rule 21 or rule 22 shall, upon receipt thereof, proceed as if it had been issued by such Court and shall then return the summons to the Court of issue, together with the record (if any) of its proceedings with regard thereto.

Rule 24 Service on defendant in Prison

Where the defendant is confined in a prison, the summons shall be delivered or sent [by post or by such courier service as may be approved by the High Court, by fax message or by Electronic Mail service or by any other means as may be provided by the rules made by the High Court][105] to the officer in charge of the prison for service on the defendant.

---

[105] Subs, by Act No. 46 of 1999, section 15 (*with effect from* 1-7-2002) for certain words

Rule 25 Service where defendant resides out of India and has no agent

Where the defendant resides out of [India] and has no agent in [India] empowered to accept service, the summons shall be addressed to the defendant at the place where he is residing and sent to him [by post or by such courier service as may be approved by the High Court, by fax message or by Electronic Mail service or by any other means as may be provided by the rules made by the High Court], if there is postal communication between such place and the place where the Court is situate :

[Provided that where any such defendant [resides in Bangladesh or Pakistan] the summons, together with a copy thereof, may be sent for service on the defendant, to any Court in that country (not being the High Court) having jurisdiction in the place where the defendant resides:

Provided further that where any such defendant is a public officer [in Bangladesh or Pakistan (not belonging to the Bangladesh or, as the case may be, Pakistan military naval or air forces)] or is servant of a railway company or local authority in that country, the summons, together with a copy thereof, may be sent for service on the defendant, to such officer or authority in that country as the Central Government may, by notification in the Official Gazette, specify in this behalf.]

Rule 26 Service in foreign territory through Political agent or Court

Where –

(a) in the exercise of any foreign jurisdiction vested in the Central Government, a Political Agent has been appointed, or a Court has been established or continued, with power to serve a summons, issued by a Court under this Code, in any foreign territory in which the defendant actually and voluntarily resides, carries on business or personally works for gain, or

(b) the Central Government has, by notification in the Official Gazette, declared, in respect of any Court situate in any such territory and not established or continued in the exercise of any such jurisdiction as aforesaid, that service by such Court of any summons issued by a Court under this Code shall be deemed to be valid service, the summons may be sent to such Political Agent or Court, by post, or otherwise, or if so directed by the Central Government, through the Ministry of that Government dealing with foreign affairs, or in such other manner as may be specified by the Central Government for the purpose of being served upon the defendant: and, if the Political Agent or Court returns the summons with an endorsement purporting to have been made by such Political Agent or by the Judge or other officer of the Court to the effect that the summons has been served on the defendant in the manner hereinbefore directed, such endorsement shall be deemed to be evidence of service.

Rule 26-A Summonses to be sent to officers of foreign countries

Where the Central Government has, by notification in the Official Gazette, declared in respect of any foreign territory that summonses to be served on defendants actually and voluntarily residing or carrying on business or personally working for gain in that foreign territory may be sent to an officer of the Government of the foreign territory specified by the Central Government, the summonses may be sent to such officer, through the Ministry of the Government of India dealing with foreign affairs or in such other manner as may be specified by the Central Government; and if such officer returns any such summons with an endorsement purporting to have been made by him that the summons has been served on the defendant, such endorsement shall be deemed to be evidence of service.]

Rule 27 Service on civil public office or on servant of railway company or local authority

Where the defendant is a public officer (not belonging to [the Indian] military, [naval or air] forces) or is the servant of a railway company or local authority, the Court may, if it appears to it that the summons may be most conveniently so served, send it for service on the defendant to the head of the office in which he is employed together with a copy to be retained by the defendant.

Rule 28 Service on soldiers, sailors or airmen

Where the defendant is a soldier, [sailor] [or airman], the Court shall send the summons for service to his commanding officer together with a copy to be retained by the defendant.

Rule 29 Duty of person to whom summons is delivered or sent for service

(1) Where a summons is delivered or sent to any person for service under rule 24, rule 27 or rule 28, such person shall be bound to serve it if possible and to return it under his signature, with the written acknowledgement of the defendant, and such signature shall be deemed to be evidence of service.

(2) Where from any cause service is impossible, the summons shall be returned to the Court with a full statement of such cause and of the steps taken to procure service, and such statement shall be deemed to be evidence of non-service.

Rule 30 Substitution of letter for summons

(1) The Court may, notwithstanding anything hereinbefore contained, substitute for a summons a letter signed by the Judge or such officer as he may appoint in this behalf, where the defendant is, in the opinion of the Court, of a rank entitling him to such mark of consideration.

(2) A letter substituted under sub-rule (1) shall contain all the particulars required to be stated in a summons, and, subject to the provisions of sub-rule (3), shall be treated in all respects as a summons.

(3) A letter so substituted may be sent to the defendant by spot or by a special messenger selected by the Court, or in any other manner which the Court thinks fit; and where the defendant has an agent empowered to accept service, the letter may be delivered or sent to such agent.

O R D E R IX: APPEARANCE OF PARTIES AND CONSEQUENCE OF NON-APPEARANCE

Rule 1 Parties to appear on day fixed in summons for defendant to appear and answer

Rule 2 Dismissal of suit where summons not served in consequence of the plaintiff's failure to pay cost

Where on the day so fixed it is found that the summons has not been served upon the defendant in consequence of the failure of the plaintiff to pay the court-fee or postal charges, if any, chargeable for such service, or failure to present copies of the plaint as required by rule 9 of Order VII, the Court may make an order that the suit be dismissed:

Provided that no such order shall be made, if, notwithstanding such failure, the defendant attends in person or by agent when he is allowed to appear by agent on the day fixed for him to appear and answer.

Rule 3 Where neither party appears, suit to be dismissed

Where neither party appears when the suit is called on for hearing, the Court may make an order that the suit be dismissed.

Rule 4 Plaintiff may bring fresh suit or Court may restore suit to file

Where a suit is dismissed under rule 2 or rule 3, the plaintiff may (subject to the law of limitation) bring a fresh suit, or he may apply for an order to set the dismissal aside, and if he satisfies the Court that there was sufficient cause for [such failure as is referred to in rule 2], or for his non-appearance, as the case may be, the Court shall make an order setting aside the dismissal and shall appoint a day for proceeding with the suit.

Rule 5 Dismissal of suit where plaintiff, after summons returned unserved, fails for one month to apply for fresh summons

(1) [Where after a summons has been issued to the defendant, or to one of several defendants, and returned unserved the plaintiff fails, for a periods of [seven days] from the date

of the return made to the Court by the officer ordinarily certifying to the Court returns made by the serving officers, to apply for the issue of a fresh summons the Court shall make an order that the suit be dismissed as against such defendant, unless the plaintiff has within the said period satisfied the Court that--

a. he has failed after using his best endeavours to discover the residence of the defendant, who has not been served, or

b. such defendant is avoiding service of process, or

c. there is any other sufficient cause for extending the time, in which case the Court may extend the time for making such application for such period as it thinks fit.]

(2) In such case the plaintiff may (subject to the law of limitation) bring a fresh suit.

Rule 6 Procedure when only Plaintiff appears

(1) Where the plaintiff appears and the defendant does not appear when the suit is called on for hearing, then-

(a) [When summons duly served-if it is proved that the summons was duly served, the Court may make an order that the suit shall be heard ex pane.]

(b) When summons not duly served-if it is not proved that the summons was duly served, the Court shall direct a second summons to be issued and served on the defendant;

(c) When summons served but not in due time-if it is proved that the summons was served on the defendant, but not in sufficient time to enable him to appear and answer on the day fixed in the summons, the Court shall postpone the hearing of the suit to future day to be fixed by the Court, and shall direct notice of such day to be given to the defendant.

(2) Where it is owing to the plaintiff's default that the summons was not duly served or was not served in sufficient time, the Court shall order the plaintiff to pay the costs occasioned by the postponement.

Rule 7 Procedure where Defendant appears on day of adjourned hearing and assigns good cause for previous non-appearance

Where the Court has adjourned the hearing of the suit ex parte and the defendant, at or before such hearing, appears and assigns good cause for his previous non-appearance, he may, upon such terms as the Court directs as to costs or otherwise, be heard in answer to the suit as if he had appeared on the day, fixed for his appearance.

Rule 8 Procedure when defendant ONLY APPEARS

Where the defendant appears and the plaintiff does not appear when the suit is called on for hearing, the Court shall make an order that the suit be dismissed, unless the defendant admits the claim or part thereof, in which case the Court shall pass a decree against the defendant upon such admission, and, where part only of the claim has been admitted, shall dismiss the suit so far as it relates to the remainder.

Rule 9 Decree against plaintiff by default bars fresh suit

(1) Where a suit is wholly or partly dismissed under rule 8, the plaintiff shall be precluded from bringing a fresh suit in respect of the same cause of action. But he may apply for an order to set the dismissal aside, and if he satisfies the Court that there was sufficient cause for his non-appearance when the suit was called on for hearing, the Court shall make an order setting aside the dismissal upon such terms as to costs or otherwise as it thinks fit. and shall appoint a day for proceeding with suit.

(3) No order shall be made under this rule unless notice of the application has been served on the opposite party.

Rule 10 Procedure in case of non-attendance of one or more of several plaintiffs

Where there are more plaintiffs than one, and one or more of them appear, and the others do not appear, the Court may, at the instance of the plaintiff or plaintiffs appearing, permit the suit to proceed in the same way as if all the plaintiffs had appeared, or make such order as it thinks fit.

Rule 11 Procedure in case of non-attendance of one or more of several defendants

Where there are more defendants than one, and one or more of them appear, and the others do not appear, the suit shall proceed, and the Court shall, at the time of pronouncing judgment, make such order as it thinks fit with respect to the defendants who do not appear.

Rule 12 Consequence of non-attendance, without sufficient cause shown, of party ordered to appear in person

Where a plaintiff or defendant, who has been ordered to appear in person, does not appear in person, or show sufficient cause to the satisfaction of the Court for failing so to appear, he shall be subject to all the provisions of the foregoing rules applicable to plaintiffs and defendants, respectively who do not appear.

Rule 13 Setting aside decree ex parte against defendant

In any case in which a decree is passed ex parte against a defendant, he may apply to the Court by which the decree was passed for an order to set it aside; and if he satisfies the Court that the summons was not duly served, or that he was prevented by any sufficient cause from appearing when the suit was called on for hearing, the Court shall make an order setting aside the decree as against him upon such terms as to costs, payment into Court or otherwise as it thinks fit, and shall appoint a day for proceeding with the suit;

Provided that where the decree is of such a nature that it cannot be set aside as against such defendant only it may be set aside as against all or any of the other defendants also:

[106][Provided further that no Court shall set aside a decree passed ex parte merely on the ground that there has been an irregularity in the service of summons, if it is satisfied that the defendant had notice of the date of hearing and had sufficient time to appear and answer the plaintiff s claim]

[107][Explanation.-Where there has been an appeal against a decree passed *ex parte* under this rule, and the appeal has been disposed of on any ground other than the ground that the appellant has withdrawn the appeal, no application shall lie under this rule for setting aside that ex parte decree.]

Rule 14 No decree to be set aside without notice to opposite party

No decree shall be set aside on any such application as aforesaid unless notice thereof has been served on the opposite party.

ORDER XI: DISCOVERY AND INSPECTION

Rule 12 Application for discovery of documents

Any party may, without filing any affidavit, apply to the Court for an order directing any other party to any suit to make discovery on oath of the documents which are or have been in his possession or power, relating to any matter in question therein. On the hearing of such application the Court may either refuse or adjourn the same, if satisfied that such discovery is not necessary, or not necessary at that stage of the suit, or make such order, either generally or limited to certain classes of documents, as may, in its discretion be thought fit:

Provided that discovery shall not be ordered when and so far as the Court shall be of opinion that it is not necessary either for disposing fairly of the suit or for saving costs.

---

[106] Added by Act No. 104 of 1976 (*with effect from* 1-2-1977).
[107] Added by Act No. 104 of 1976 (*with effect from* 1-2-1977).

Rule 13 Affidavit of documents

The affidavit to be made by a party against whom such order as is mentioned in the last preceding rule has been made, shall specify which (if any) of the documents therein mentioned the objects to produce, and it shall be in Form No. 5 in Appendix C, with such variations as circumstances may require.

Rule 14 Production of documents

It shall be lawful for the Court, at any time during the pendency of any suit, to order the production by any party thereto, upon oath of such of the documents in his possession or power, relating to any matter in question in such suit, as the Court shall think right; and the Court may deal with such documents, when produced, in such manner as shall appear just.

Rule 15 Inspection of documents referred to in pleadings or affidavits

Every party to a suit shall be entitled [at or before the settlement of issues] to give notice to any other party, in whose pleadings or affidavits reference is made to any document [or who has entered any document in any list annexed to his pleadings] or produce such document for the inspection of the party giving such notice, or of his pleader, and to permit him or them to take copies thereof; and any party not complying with such notice shall not afterwards be at liberty to put any such document in evidence on his behalf in such suit unless he shall satisfy the Court that such document relates only to his own title, he being a defendant to the suit, or that he had some other cause or excuse with the Court shall deem sufficient for not complying with such notice, in which case the Court may allow the same to be put in evidence on such terms as to costs an otherwise as the Court shall think fit.

Rule 16 Notice to produce

Notice to any party to produce any documents referred to in his pleading or affidavits shall be in Form No. 7 in Appendix C, with such variations as circumstances may require.

Rule 17 Time for inspection when notice given

The party to whom such notice is given shall, within ten days from the receipt of such notice, deliver to the party giving the same a notice stating a time within three days from the delivery thereof at which the documents, or such of them as he does not object to produce, may be inspected at the office of his pleader, or in the case of bankers books or other books of account or books in constant use for the purposes of any trade or business, at their usual place of custody, and stating which (if any) of the documents he objects to produce, and on what ground. Such notice shall be in Form No. 8 in Appendix C, with such variations as circumstances may require.

Rule 18 Order for inspection

(1) Where the party served with notice under rule 15 omits to give such notice of a time for inspection or objects to give inspection, or offers inspection elsewhere than at the office of his pleader, the Court may, on the application of the party desiring it, make an order for inspection in such place and in such manner as it may think fit:

Provided that the order shall not be made when and so far as the Court shall be of opinion that, it is not necessary either for disposing fairly of the suit or for saving costs.

(1) Any application to inspect documents, except such as are referred to in the pleadings, particulars or affidavits of the party against whom the application is made or disclosed in his affidavit of documents, shall be founded upon an affidavit showing of what documents inspection is sought, that the party applying is entitled to inspect them, and that they are in the possession or power of the other party. The Court shall not make such order for inspection of such documents when and so far as the Court shall be of opinion that it is not necessary either for disposing fairly of the suit or for saving costs.

ORDER XIII: PRODUCTION, IMPOUNDING AND RETURN OF DOCUMENTS

Rule 3 Rejection of irrelevant or inadmissible documents

The Court may at any stage of the suit reject any document which it considers irrelevant or otherwise inadmissible, recording the grounds of such rejection.

Rule 4 Endorsements on documents admitted in evidence

(1) Subject to the provisions of the next following sub-rule, there shall be endorsed on every document which has been admitted in evidence in the suit the following particulars, namely:-

a) the number and title of the suit,

b) the name of the person producing the document,

c) the date on which it was produced, and

d) a statement of its having been so admitted, and the endorsement shall be signed or initialed by the Judge.

(2) Where a document so admitted is an entry in a book, account or record, and a copy thereof has been substituted for the original under the next following rule, the particulars aforesaid shall be endorsed on the copy and the endorsement thereon shall be signed or initialled by the Judge.

Rule 5 endorsements on copies of admitted entries in books

1) Save in so far as is otherwise provided by the Bankers' Books Evidence Act, 1891 (18 of 1891) where a document admitted in evidence in the suit is an entry in a letter-book or a shop-book or other account in current use, the party on whose behalf the book or account is produced may furnish a copy of the entry.

2) Where such a document is an entry in a public record produced from a public office or by a public officer, or an entry in a book or account belonging to a person other than a party on whose behalf the book or account is

produced, the Court may require a copy of the entry to be furnished--

a) where the record, book or account is produced on behalf of a party, then by that party, or

b) where the record, book or account is produced in obedience to an order of the Court acting of its own motion, then by either or any party.

3) Where a copy of an entry is furnished under the foregoing provisions of this rule, the Court shall, after accusing the copy to be examined, compared and certified in manner mentioned in rule 17 of Order VII, mark the entry and cause the book account or record in which it occurs to be returned to the person producing it.

Rule 6 Endorsements on documents rejected as inadmissible in evidence

When a document relied on as evidence by either party is considered by the Court to be inadmissible in evidence, there shall be endorsed thereon the particulars mentioned in clauses (a), (b), and (c) of rule 4, sub-rule (1), together with a statement of its having been rejected, and the endorsement shall be signed or initialled by the Judge.

Rule 7 Recording of admitted and return of rejected documents

1) Every document which has been admitted in evidence or a copy thereof where a copy has been substituted for the original under rule 5, shall form part of the record of the suit.

(2) Documents not admitted in evidence shall not form part of the record and shall be returned to the persons respectively producing them.

Rule 8 Court may order any document to be impounded

Notwithstanding anything contained in rule 5 or rule 7 of this Order or in rule 17 of Order VII, the Court may, if it sees sufficient cause, direct any document or book produced before it in any suit to be impounded and kept in the custody of an officer of the Court, for such period and subject to such conditions as the Court think fit.

Rule 9 Return of admitted documents

1) Any person, whether a party to the suit or not, desirous of receiving back any document produced by him in the suit and placed on the record shall, unless the document is impounded under rule 8, be entitled to receive back the same,--

   (a) where the suit is one in which an appeal is not allowed, when the suit has been disposed of, and

   (b) where the suit is one in which an appeal is allowed, when the Court is satisfied that the time for preferring an appeal has elapsed and that no appeal has been preferred or, if an appeal has been preferred, when the appeal has been disposed of:

[Provided that a document may be returned at any time earlier than that prescribed by this rule if the person applying therefore-

   (a) delivers to the proper officer for being substituted for the original,--

      (i) in the case of a party to the suit, a certified copy, and

      (ii) in the case of any other person, an ordinary copy which has been examined, compared and certified in the manner mentioned in sub-rule (2) of rule 17 of Order VII, and

   (b) undertakes to produce the original, if required to do so :]

Provided also, that no document shall be returned with, by force of the decree, has become wholly void or useless.

   (2) On the return of a document admitted in evidence, a receipt shall be given by the person receiving it.

Rule 10 Court may send for papers form its own records or from other Courts

(1) The Court may of its own motion, and may in its discretion upon the application of any of the parties to a suit, send for, either from its own records or from any other suit or proceedings, and inspect the same.

(2) Every application made under this rule (unless the Court otherwise directs) be supported by an affidavit showing how the record is material to the suit in which the application is made, and that the applicant cannot without unreasonable delay or expense obtain a duly authenticated copy of the record or of such portion thereof as the applicant requires, or that the production of the original is necessary for the purposes of justice.

(3) Nothing contained in this rule shall be deemed to enable the Court to use in evidence any document which under the law of evidence would be inadmissible in the suit.

ORDER XVI. SUMMONING AND ATTENDANCE OF WITNESSES

Rule 1 List of witnesses and summons to witnesses

[1. List of witnesses and summons to witnesses

(1) On or before such date as the Court may appoint, and not later than fifteen days after the date on which the issues are settled, the parties shall present in Court a list of witnesses whom they propose to call either to give evidence or to produce documents and obtain summonses to such person for their attendance in Court.

(2) A party desirous of obtaining any summons for the attendance of any person shall file in Court an application stating therein the purpose for which the witness is proposed to be summoned.

(4) The Court may, for reasons to be recorded, permit a party to call, whether by summoning through Court or otherwise, any witness, other than those whose names appear in the list referred to in sub-rule (1), if such part

shows sufficient cause for the omission to mention the name of such witness in the said list.

(5) Subject to the provisions of sub-rule (2), summonses referred to in this rule may be obtained by the parties on an application to the Court or to such officer as may be appointed by the [Court in this behalf within five days of presenting the list of witnesses under sub-rule (1)].

Rule 1-A Production of witnesses without summons

A subject to the provisions of sub-rule (3) of rule 1, and party to the suit may, without applying for summons under rule 1, bring any witness to give evidence or to produce documents.

Rule 2 Expenses of witness to be paid into Court on applying for summons

(1) The party applying for a summons shall, before the summons is granted and within a period to be fixed [which shall not be later than seven days from the date of making application under sub-rule (4) of rule 1], pay into Court such a sum of money as appears to the Court to be sufficient to defray the travelling and other expenses of the person summoned in passing to and from the Court in which he is required to attend, and for one day's attendance.

(2) Experts—In determining the amount payable under this rule, the Court may, in the case of any person summoned to give evidence as an expert, allow reasonable remuneration for the time occupied both in giving evidence and in performing any work of an expert character necessary for the case.

(3) Scale of expenses—Where the Court is subordinate to High Court, regard shall be had, in fixing the scale of such expenses to a any rules made in that behalf.

i) [(4)] Expenses to be directly paid to witnesses—Where the summons is served directly by the party on a witness, the expenses referred to in sub-rule (1) shall be paid to the witness by the party or his agent.]

Rule 4 Procedure where insufficient sum paid in

(1) Where it appears to the Court or to such officer as it appoints in this behalf that the sum paid into Court is not sufficient to cover such expenses or reasonable remuneration, the Court may direct such further sum to be paid to the person summoned as appears to be necessary on that account, and, in case of default in payment, may order such sum to be levied by attachment and sale of the movable property of the party obtaining the summons; or the Court may discharge the person summoned without requiring him to give evidence; or may both order such levy and discharge such person as aforesaid.

(2) Expenses of witnesses detained more than one day— Where it is necessary to detain the person summoned for a longer period than one day, the Court may, from time to time, order the party at whose instance he was summoned to pay into Court such sum as is sufficient to defray the expenses of his detention for such further period, and, in default of such deposit being made, may order such sum to be levied by attachment and sale of the movable property of such party; or the Court may discharge the person summoned without requiring him to give evidence, or may other order such levy and discharge such person as aforesaid.

Rule 5 Time, place and purpose of attendance to be specified in summons

Every summons for the attendance of a person to give evidence or to produce a document shall specify the time and place at which he is required to attend, and also whether his attendance is required for the purpose of giving evidence or to produce a document, or for both purposes; and any particular document, which the person summoned is called on to produce, shall be described in the summons with reasonable accuracy.

Rule 6 Summons to produce documents

Any person may be summoned to produce a document, without being summoned to give evidence, and any person summoned merely to produce a document shall be deemed to have complied with the summons if he causes such document to be produced instead of attending personally to produce the same.

Rule 7 Power to require persons present in Court to give evidence or produce documents

Any person present in Court may be required by the Court to give evidence or to produce any document then and there in his possession or power.

Rule 8 Summons how served

Every summons[under this Order, not being a summons delivered to a party for service under rule 7A,] shall be served as nearly as may be in the same manner as a summons to a defendant and the rules in Order V as to proof of service shall apply in the case of all summonses served under this rule.

Rule 9 Time for serving summons

Service shall in all cases be made a sufficient time before the time specified in the summons for the attendance of the person summoned, to allow him a reasonable time for preparation and for travelling to the place at which his attendance is required.

Rule 10 Procedure where witness fails to comply with summons

(1) **Where a person to whom a summons has been issued either to attend to give evidence or to produce a document, fails to attend or to produce the document in compliance with such summons, the Court—**

(a) shall, if the certificate of the serving officer has not been verified by affidavit, or if service of the summons has been effected by a party or his agent, or

(b) may, if the certificate of the serving officer has been so verified, examine on oath the serving officer or the party or his agent, as the case may be, who has effected service, or cause him to be so examined by any Court, touching the service or non-service of the summons.

(2) Where the Court sees reason to believe that such evidence or production is material, and that such person has, without lawful excuse, failed to attend or to produce the document in compliance with such summons or has intentionally avoided service, it may issue a proclamation requiring him to attend to give evidence or to produce the document at a time and place to be named therein; and a copy of such proclamation shall be affixed on the outer door or other conspicuous part of the house in which he ordinarily resides.

(3) In view of or at the time of issuing such proclamation, or at any time afterwards, the Court may, in its discretion, issue a warrant, either with or without bail, for the arrest of such person, and may make an order for the attachment of his property to such amount as it thinks fit, not exceeding the amount of the costs of attachment and of any fine which may be imposed under rule 12 :

Provided that no Court of Small Causes shall make an order for the attachment of immovable property.

Rule 11 If witness appears attachment may be withdrawn

Where at any time after the attachment of his property, such person appears and satisfies the Court—

(a) that he did not, without lawful excuse, fail to comply with the summons or intentionally avoid service, and

(b) where he has failed to attend at the time and place named in a proclamation issued under the last proceeding rule, that he had no notice of such proclamation in time to attend.

The Court shall direct that the property be released from attachment, and shall make such order as to the costs of the attachment as it thinks fit.

Rule 12 Procedure if witness fails to appear

(1) The Court may, where such person does not appear, or appears but fails so to satisfy the Court, impose upon him such fine not exceeding five hundred rupees as it thinks

fit, having regard to his condition in life and all the circumstances of the case, and may order his property, or any part thereof, to the attached and sold or, if already attached under rule 10, to be sold for the purpose of satisfying all costs to such attachment, together with the amount of the said fine, if any:

Provided that, if the person whose attendance is required pays into Court the Costs and fine aforesaid, the Court shall order the property to be released from attachment.

(2) [Notwithstanding that the Court has not issued a proclamation under sub-rule (2) of rule 10, nor issued a warrant nor ordered attachment under sub-rule (3) of that rule, the Court may impose fine under sub-rule (1) of this rule after giving notice to such person to show cause why the fine should not be imposed.]

Rule 13 Mode of attachment

The provisions with regard to the attachment and sale of property in the execution of a decree shall, so far as they are applicable, be deemed to apply to any attachment and sale under this Order as if the person whose property is so attached were a judgment-debtor.

Rule 14 Court may of its own accord summon as witnesses strangers to suit

Subject to the provisions of this Code as to attendance and appearance and to any law for the time being in force, where the Court at any time thinks it necessary [to examine any person, including a party to the suit] and not called as witness by a party to the suit, the Court may, of its own motion, cause such person to be summoned as a witness to give evidence, or to produce any document in his possession on a day to be appointed, and may examine him as a witness or require him to produce such document.

Rule 15 Duty of persons summoned to give evidence or produce documents

Subject as last aforesaid, whoever is summoned to appear and give evidence in a suit shall attend at the time and place named in the summons for that purpose, and whoever is summoned to produce a document shall either attend to produce it, or cause it to be produced, at such time and place.

Rule 16 When they may depart

(1) A person so summoned and attending shall, unless the Court otherwise directs, attend at each hearing until the suit has been disposed of.

(2) On the application of either party and the payment through the Court of all necessary expenses (if any), the Court may require any person so summoned and attending to furnish security to attend at the next or any other hearing or until the suit is disposed of and, in default of his furnishing such security, may order him to be detained in the civil prison.

Rule 17 Application of rules 10 to 13

The provisions of rules 10 to 13 shall, so far as they are applicable, be deemed to apply to any person who having attended in compliance with a summons departs, without lawful excuse, in contravention of rule 16.

RULE 18 PROCEDURE WHERE WITNESS APPREHENDED CANNOT GIVE EVIDENCE OR PRODUCE DOCUMENT

Where any person arrested under a warrant is brought before the Court in custody and cannot, owing to the absence of the parties or any of them, give the evidence or produce the document which he has been summoned to give or produce, the Court may require him to give reasonable bail or other security for his appearance at such time and place as it thinks fit, on such bail or security being given, may release him, and, in default of his giving such bail or security, any order him to be detained in the civil prison.

RULE 19 NO WITNESS TO BE ORDERED TO ATTEND IN PERSON UNLESS RESIDENT WITHIN CERTAIN LIMITS

No one shall be ordered to attend in person to give evidence unless he resides—

(a) within the local limits of the Court's ordinary original jurisdiction, or

(b) without such limits but at a place less than [one hundred] or (where there is railway or steamer communication .or other established public conveyance for five-sixths of the distance between the place where he resides and the place where the Court is situate) less than [five hundred kilometers] distance from the Court house:

[Provided that where transport by air is available between the two places mentioned in this rule and the witness is paid the fare by air, he may be ordered to attend in person.]

Rule 20 Consequence of refusal of party to give evidence when called on by Court

Where any party to a suit present in Court refuses, without lawful excuse, when required by the Court, to give evidence or to produce any document then and there in his possession or power, the Court may pronounce judgment against him or make such order in relation to the suit as it thinks fit.

Rule 21 Rules as to witnesses to apply to parties summoned

Where any party to a suit is required to give evidence or to produce a document, the provisions as to witnesses shall apply to him so for as they are applicable.

ORDER XVII. ADJOURNMENTS

Rule 1 Court may grant time and adjourn hearing

(1) [The Court may, if sufficient cause is shown, at any stage of the suit grant time to the parties or to any of them, and may from time to time adjourn the hearing of the suit for reasons to be recorded in writing:

Provided that no such adjournment shall be granted more than three times to a party during hearing of the suit.]

(2) Costs of adjournment--In every such case the Court shall fix a day for the further hearing of the suit and [shall make such orders as to costs occasioned by the adjournment or such higher costs as the court deems fit]:

[Provided that,--

(a) when the hearing of the suit has commenced, it shall be continued from day-to-day until all the witnesses in attendance have been examined, unless the Court finds that, for the exceptional reasons to be recorded by it, the adjournment of the hearing beyond the following day is necessary.

(b) no adjournment shall be granted at the request of a party, except where the circumstances are beyond the control of that party.

(c) the fact that the pleader of a party is engaged in another Court, shall not be a ground for adjournment.

(d) where the illness of a pleader or his inability to conduct the case for any reason, other than his being engaged in another Court, is put forward as a ground for adjournment, the Court shall not grant the adjournment unless it is satisfied that the party applying for adjournment could not have engaged another pleader in time.

(e) where a witness is present in Court but a party or his pleader is not present or the party or his pleader, though present in Court, is not ready to examine or cross-examine the witness, the Court may, if it thinks fit, record the statement of the witness and pass such orders as it thinks fit dispensing with the examination-in-chief or cross-examination of the witness, as the case may be, by the party or his pleader not present or not ready as aforesaid.

Rule 2 Procedure if parties fail to appear on a day fixed

Where, on any day to which the hearing of the suit is adjourned, the parties or any of them fail to appear, the Court may proceed to dispose of the suit in one of the modes directed in that behalf by Order IX or make such other order as it thinks fit.

[Explanation.-Where the evidence or a substantial portion of the evidence of any party has already been recorded and such party fails to appear on any day to which the hearing of the suit is adjourned, the Court may, in its discretion, proceed with the case as if such party were present.]

Rule 3 Court may proceed notwithstanding either party fails to produce evidence, etc.

Where any party to a suit to whom time has been granted fails to produce his evidence, or to cause the attendance of his witnesses, or to perform any other act necessary to the further progress of the suit, for which time has been allowed, [the Court may, notwithstanding such default,--

(a) if the parties are present, proceed to decide the suit forthwith, or

(b) if the parties are, or any of them is, absent, proceed under rule 2.

ORDER XVIII. HEARING OF THE SUIT AND EXAMINATION OF WITNESSES

Rule 16 Power to examine witness immediately

(1) Where a witness is about to leave the jurisdiction of the Court, or other sufficient cause is shown to the satisfaction of the Court why his evidence should be taken immediately, the Court may upon the application of any party or of the witness, at any time after the institution of the suit, take the evidence of such witness in manner herein before provided.

(3) Where such evidence is not taken forthwith and in the presence of the parties, such notice as the Court thinks sufficient, of the day fixed for the examination, shall be given to the parties.

(4) The evidence so taken shall be read over to the witness, and if he admits it to be correct, shall be signed by him,

and the Judge shall, if necessary, correct the same, and shall sign it, and it may then be read at any hearing of the suit.

Rule 17 Court may recall and examine witness

The Court may at any stage of a suit recall any witness who has been examined and may (subject to the law of evidence for the time being in force) put such questions to him as the Court thinks fit.

Rule 18 Power of Court to inspect

The Court may at any stage of a suit inspect any property or thing concerning which any question may arise [and where the Court inspects any property or thing it shall, as soon as may be practicable, make a memorandum of any relevant facts observed at such inspection and such memorandum shall form a part of the record of the suit.]

ORDER XIX. AFFIDAVITS

Rule 1 Power to order any point to be proved by affidavit

Any Court may at any time for sufficient reason order that any particular fact or facts may be proved by affidavit, or that the affidavit of any witness may be read at the hearing, on such conditions as the Court thinks reasonable :

Provided that where it appears to the Court that either party bona fide desires the production of a witness for cross-examination, and that such witness can be produced, an order shall not be made authorizing the evidence of such witness to be given by affidavit.

Rule 2 Power to order attendance of deponent for cross-examination

(1) Upon any application evidence may be given by affidavit, but the Court may, at the instance of either party, order the attendance for cross-examination of the deponent.

(2) Such attendance shall be in Court, unless the deponent is exempted from personal appearance in Court or the Court otherwise directs.

Rule 3 Matters to which affidavits shall be confined

(1) Affidavits shall be confined to such facts as the deponent is able of his own knowledge to prove, except on interlocutory applications, on which statements of his belief may be admitted, provided that the grounds thereof are stated.

(2) The costs of every affidavit which shall unnecessarily set forth matters of hearsay or argumentative matter, or copies of or extracts from document, shall (unless the Court otherwise directs) be paid by the party filing the same.

ORDER XXVI: COMMISSIONS, COMMISSIONS TO EXAMINE WITNESSES

Rule 1 Cases in which Court may issue commission to examine witness

Any Court may in any suit issue a commission for the examination on interrogatories or otherwise of any person resident within the local limits of its jurisdiction who is exempted under this Code from attending the Court or who is from sickness or infirmity unable to attend it:

[Provided that a commission for examination on interrogatories shall not be issued unless the Court, for reasons to be recorded, thinks it necessary so to do].

Explanation-The Court may, for the purpose of this rule, accept a certificate purporting to be signed by a registered medical practitioner as evidence of the sickness or infertility of any person, without calling the medical practitioner as a witness.

Rule 2 Order for commission

An order for the issue of a commission for the examination of a witness may be made by the Court either of its own motion or on the application, supported by affidavit or otherwise, of any party to the suit or of the witness to be examined.

Rule 3 Where witness resides within Court's jurisdiction

A commission for the examination of a person who resides within the local limits of the jurisdiction of the Court issuing the same may be issued to any person whom the Court thinks fit to execute it.

Rule 4 Persons for whose examination commission may issue

(1) Any Court may in any suit issue a commission [for the examination of interrogatories or otherwise of --]

(a) any person resident beyond the local limits of its jurisdiction;

(b) any person who is about to leave such limits before the date on which he is required to be examined in Court; and

(c) [any person in the service of the Government] who cannot in the opinion of the Court, attend without detriment to the public service:

[Provided that where, under rule 19 of Order XVI, a person cannot be ordered to attend a Court in person, a commission shall be issued for his examination if his evidence is considered necessary in the interests of justice:

Provided further that a commission for examination of such person on interrogatories shall not be issued unless the Court, for reasons to be recorded, thinks it necessary so to do.]

(2) Such commission may be issued to any Court, not being a High Court, within the local limits of whose jurisdiction such person resides, or to any pleader or other person whom the Court issuing the commission may appoint.

(3) The Court on issuing any commission may this rule shall direct whether the commission shall be returned to itself or to any subordinate Court.

Rule 5 Commission or request to examine witness not within India

Where any Court to which application is made for the issue of a commission for the examination B of a person residing at any place not within India is satisfied that the evidence of such person is necessary, the Court may issue such commission or a letter of request.

Rule 6 Court to examine witness pursuant to commission

Every Court receiving a commission for the examination of any person shall examine him or cause him to be examined pursuant thereto.

Rule 7 Return of commission with depositions of witnesses

Where a commission has been duly executed, it shall be returned, together with the evidence taken under it, to the Court from which it was issued, unless the order for issuing the commission has otherwise directed, in which case the commission shall be returned in terms of such order; and the commission and the returned thereto and the evidence taken under it shall [subject to the provisions of rule 8] form part of the record of the suit.

Rule 8 When depositions may be read in evidence

Evidence taken under a commission shall not be read as evidence in the suit without the consent of the party against whom the same is offered, unless--

(a) the person who gave the evidence is beyond the jurisdiction of the Court, or dead or unable from sickness or infirmity to attend to be personally examined, or exempted from personal appearance in Court or is a person in the service of the Government who cannot, in the opinion of the Court, attend without detriment to the public service, or

(b) the Court in its discretion dispenses with the proof of any of the circumstances mentioned in clause (a) and authorizes the evidence of any person being read as evidence in the suit, notwithstanding proof that the cause for taking such evidence by commission has ceased at the time of reading the same.

Rule 9 Commission to make local investigations

In any suit in which the Court deems a local investigation to be requisite or proper for the purpose of elucidating any matter in dispute, or of ascertaining the market-value of any property, or the amount of any *mesne* profits or damages or annual net profits, the Court may issue a commission to such person as it thinks fit directing him to make such investigation and to report thereon to the Court:

Provided that, where the State Government has made rules as to the persons to whom such commission shall be issued, the Court shall be bound by such rules.

Rule 10 Procedure of Commissioner

(1) The Commissioner, after such local inspection as he deems necessary and after reducing to writing the evidence taken by him, shall return such evidence, together with his report in writing signed by him, to the Court.

(2) Report and deposition to be evidence in suit. Commissioner may be examined in person--The report of the Commissioner and the evidence taken by him (but not the evidence without the report) shall be evidence in the suit and shall form part of the record; but the Court or, with the permission of the Court, any of the parties to suit may examine the Commissioner personally in open Court touching any part of the matters referred to him or mentioned in his report, or as to his report, or as to the manner in which he has made the investigation.

(3) Where the Court is for any reason dissatisfied with the proceedings of the Commissioner, it may direct such further inquiry to be made as it shall think fit.

Rule 12 Court to give Commissioner necessary instructions

(1) The Court shall furnish the Commissioner with such part of the proceedings and such instructions as appear necessary and the instructions shall distinctly specify whether the Commissioner is merely to transmit the proceedings which he may hold on the inquiry, or also to report his own opinion on the point referred for his examination.

(2) Proceedings and report to be evidence. Court may direct further inquiry--The proceedings and report (if any) of the Commissioner shall be evidence in the suit, but where the Court has reason to be dissatisfied with them, it may direct such further inquiry as it shall think fit.

Rule 15 Expenses of commission to be paid into Court

Before issuing any commission under this Order, the Court may order such sum (if any) as it thinks reasonable for the expenses of the commission to be, within a time to be fixed, paid into Court by the party at whose instance or for whose benefit the commission is issued.

Rule 16 Powers of Commissioners

Any Commissioner appointed under this Order may, unless otherwise directed by the order of appointment,--

(a) examine the parties themselves and any witness whom they or any of them may produce, and any other person whom the Commissioner thinks proper to call upon to give evidence in the matter referred to him;

(b) call for and examine documents and other things relevant to the subject of inquiry;

(c) at any reasonable time enter upon or into any land or building mentioned in the order.

Rule 16-A Questions objected to before the Commissioner

(1) Where any question put to a witness is objected to by a party or his pleader in proceedings before a Commissioner appointed under this Order, the Commissioner shall take down the question, the answer, the objections and the name of the party or, as the case may be, the pleader so objecting:

Provided that the Commissioner shall not take down the answer to a question which is objected to on the ground of privilege but may continue with the examination of the witness, leaving the party to get the question of privilege decided by the Court, and, where the Court decides that there is no question of privilege, the witness may be recalled by the Commissioner and examined by him or the witness may be examined by the Court with regard to the question which was objected to on the ground of privilege.

(2) No answer taken down under sub-rule (1) shall be read was evidence in the suit except by the order of the Court.

Rule 17 Attendance and examination of witnesses before Commissioner

(1) The provisions of this Code relating to the summoning, attendance and examination of witnesses, and to the remuneration of, and penalties to be imposed upon, witnesses, shall apply to persons required to give evidence or to produce documents under this Order whether the commission in execution of which they are so required has been issued by a Court situate within or by a Court situate beyond the limits of [India], and for the purposes of this rule the Commissioner shall be deemed to be a Civil Court:

[Provided that when the Commissioner is not a Judge of a Civil Court he shall not be competent to impose penalties; but such penalties may be imposed on the application of such Commissioner by the Court by which the commission was issued.]

(2) A Commissioner may apply to any Court (not being a High Court) within the local limits on whose jurisdiction a witness resides for the issue of any process which he may find it necessary to issue to or against such witness, and such Court may, in its discretion, issue such process as it considers reasonable and proper.

Rule 18 Parties to appear before Commissioner

(1) Where a commission is issued under this Order, the Court shall direct that the parties to the suit shall appear before the Commissioner in person or by their agents or pleaders.

(2) Where all or any of the parties do not so appear, the Commissioner may proceed in their absence.

Rule 18-B Court to fix a time for return of commission

The Court issuing a commission shall fix a date on or before which the commission shall be returned to it after execution, and the date so fixed shall not be extended except where the Court, for reasons to be recorded, is satisfied that there is sufficient cause for extending the date.

CHAPTER 9
Relevant provisions of Indian Penal Code

Many quasi-judicial proceedings pertaining to various *tribunals* (Central Administrative Tribunal, The Armed Forces Tribunal, The National Green Tribunal, The Runway Claims Tribunal, Appellate Tribunal under the Energy Conservation Act 2001, Employees' Provident Funds Appellate Tribunal, Appellate Tribunal under the Competition Act 2002, etc), *commissions* (The Appropriate Commission under the Electricity Act, 2003, Central and State Information Commissions, Disciplinary Commission of the Bar Council under the Advocates Act 1961, etc), *boards* (The Copyright Board under the Copyright Act 1957 etc), the Special Director(Appeals) under the Foreign Exchange Management Act 1999, any proceedings before the *Lok Adalat* under the Legal Services Authority Act 1987 etc are deemed to be judicial proceedings within the meaning of Section 193, 228 and for the purpose of Section 196 of the Indian Penal Code (45 of 1860).

Interestingly, the term 'judicial proceeding' is not defined in the Indian Penal Code. It is defined under Section 4(m) of the Criminal Procedure Code which reads, 'Judicial proceedings includes any proceedings in the course of which evidence is or may be legally taken on oath.' Again, the term 'Court' is not defined either in the Criminal Procedure Code or in the Indian Penal Code. To obviate the ambiguity and to safeguard the quasi-judicial proceedings of tribunals/boards/commissions/statutory authorities, special provisions are usually made deeming such quasi-judicial proceedings to be 'judicial proceedings' within the meaning of Section 193, 196 and 228 of the IPC to make use of these safe-guard provisions.

Let us first look into Section 193 and 196 of IPC. Section 193 and 196 occur in Chapter XI, IPC which deals with false evidence and offences against public justice. Section 193 punishes the giving or fabricating of false evidence and section 196 punishes the using of evidence known to be false.

Sub-Section (2) of Section 7-A provides, *inter alia*, that an inquiry under sub-section (1) of Section 7A shall be deemed to be a judicial proceedings within the meaning of Sections 193, 228 and for the purpose of Section 196 of the Indian Penal Code. It is thus clear that while a Provident Fund Commissioner exercises his powers under Section 7A(1), the proceedings held by him are judicial proceedings for the purposes of the three sections of the Indian Penal Code mentioned in sub-section (2) of Section 7A.

SECTION 193 OF IPC: PUNISHMENT FOR FALSE EVIDENCE

Whoever intentionally gives false evidence in any stage of a judicial proceeding, or fabricates false evidence for the purpose of being used in any stage of a judicial proceeding, shall be punished with imprisonment of either description for a term which may extend to seven years, and shall also be liable to fine, and whoever intentionally gives or fabricates false evidence in any other case, shall be punished with imprisonment of either description for a term which may extend to three years, and shall also be liable to fine.

Explanation 1

A trial before a Court-martial; is a judicial proceeding.

Explanation 2

An investigation directed by law preliminary to a proceeding before a Court of Justice, is a stage of a judicial proceeding, though that investigation may not take place before a Court of Justice.

Illustration

A, in an enquiry before a Magistrate for the purpose of ascertaining whether Z ought to be committed for trial, makes on oath a statement which he knows to be false. As this enquiry is a stage of a judicial proceeding, A has given false evidence.

Explanation 3

An investigation directed by a Court of Justice, according to law, and conducted under the authority of a Court of Justice, is a stage of a judicial proceeding, though that investigation may not take place before a Court of Justice.

Illustration

A, in any enquiry before an officer deputed by a Court of Justice to ascertain on the spot the boundaries of land, makes on oath a statement which he knows to be false. As this enquiry is a stage of a judicial proceeding. A has given false evidence.

Giving or Fabricating False Evidence – Meaning of:

A person is said to give false evidence when he makes any statement, verbally or otherwise, which is false or which he either knows or believes to be false or does not believe to be true. This statement should, however, come from that person –

(i) who is legally bound by an oath to state the truth, or

(ii) (ii) who is legally bound by an express provision of law to state the truth, or

(iii) who is bound by law to make a declaration upon any subject.

Similarly, a person is said to have fabricated false evidence when that evidence is deliberately intended to mislead the authority to arrive at an erroneous opinion/wrong conclusion. The following incidences may be categorized into the offence of fabricating false evidences, for example.

(i) making any false entry in any book of accounts/records etc

(ii) making a document containing a false statement, or

(iii) doctoring the records , with the intention that the same may appear in evidence in a quasi-judicial proceedings and mislead the authority to entertain an erroneous opinion.

Section 193 of the Indian Penal Code, with which we are concerned here, provides for punishment for intentionally giving false evidence. It consists of two parts; the first part deals, inter alia, with false evidence intentionally given in any stage of a judicial proceeding108, and prescribes that the person found guilty of having given such false evidence in a judicial proceeding shall be punished with imprisonment of either description for a term which may extent to seven years, and shall also be liable to fine.

The second part deals with cases where false evidence has been intentionally given in any other case, and it prescribes the maximum sentence of three years as well as fine. In other words, if the false evidence has been intentionally given in any judicial proceeding, the sentence awardable is higher than that where false evidence is intentionally given in proceedings which are not judicial.

Here, Section 7A (2) of the EPF & MP Act, 1952 makes a proceedings before a Provident Fund Commissioner held under Section 7A (1), a judicial proceeding for the purposes of Section 193 IPC and it means that if an offence of giving false evidence is proved to have been committed by a person in a proceeding before the Section 7A authority, he would be liable for the higher sentence awardable under the first part of Section 193, i.e., 7 years imprisonment with fine.

SECTION 196 OF IPC: USING EVIDENCE KNOWN TO BE FALSE

Whoever corruptly uses or attempts to use as true or genuine evidence any evidence which he knows to be false or fabricated, shall be punished in the same manner as if he gave or fabricated false evidence.

---

[108] Interestingly, the expression 'judicial proceedings' is not defined under the Indian Penal Code, but it is defined under Section 4(m) of the Criminal Procedure Code

SECTION 228 OF IPC: INTENTIONAL INSULT OR INTERRUPTION TO PUBLIC SERVANT SITTING IN JUDICIAL PROCEEDING

Whoever intentionally offers any insult, or causes any interruption to any public servant, while such public servant is sitting in any stage of a judicial proceeding, shall be punished with simple imprisonment for a term which may extend to six months, or with fine which may extend to one thousand rupees, or with both.

It is a non-cognizable[109], bailable offence for which a trial can be conducted by the Court in which the offence is committed subject to the provisions of Chapter XXVI of Cr.P.C. It is a non-compoundable offence, ie, it cannot be combined with other offences, if any.

The object of the above section is to preserve the prestige and dignity of the quasi-judicial officers [personally] and those of the Offices they occupy, and to punish a person who intentionally insults the officer administering justice. Insult or interruption to a Provident Fund Commissioner would be punishable in terms of Section 7A(2) of the EPF & MP Act, 1952 read with Section 228 of the IPC, if such insult/interruption is offered intentionally by any person while the Commissioner is sitting for the disposal of proceedings under the Act. Necessary interval between two hearings in sequence may also be deemed to be part of the judicial proceedings, for this purpose.

It would be prudent to mention here that for the offences under Sections 193 and 196 of IPC, there could be no prosecution with the sanction of the Court concerned in writing.

---

[109] In Andhra Pradesh offence under section 228 is cognizable. [Vide A.P.G.O. Ms. No. 732, dated 5th December, 1991].

Nature of Offence committed	Arrest without Warrant or not	Whether a warrant Or a summons be issued at the first instance	Bailable or not	Compound-able or not
Under Section 193 of IPC – Giving or fabricating false evidence in a judicial proceeding	No arrest without a warrant	Warrant	Bailable	Un-compound-able
Under Section 196 IPC using in a judicial proceedings evidence known to be false or fabricated	No arrest without a warrant	Warrant	Bailable	Un-compound-able
Under Section 228 IPC – Intentional insult or interruption to a public servant sitting in any stage of judicial proceeding	No arrest without a warrant	Summons	Bailable	Un-compound-able

CIVIL PRISON: DETENTION AND RELEASE

Section 58 of the Code of Civil Procedure deals with the detention and release of persons in Civil Prison. It reads,

(1) Every person detained in the civil prison in execution of a decree shall be so detained,--

(a) where the decree is for the payment of a sum of money exceeding [2][five thousand rupees], for a period not exceeding three months, and

(b) [3][where the decree is for the payment of a sum of money exceeding two thousand rupees, but not exceeding five thousand rupees, for a period not exceeding six weeks :]

Provided that he shall be released from such detention before the expiration of the [4][said period of detention]--

(i) on the amount mentioned in the warrant for his detention being paid to the officer in charge of the civil prison, or

(ii) on the decree against him being otherwise fully satisfied, or

(iii) on the request of the person on whose application he has been so detained, or

(iv) on the omission by the person, on whose application he has been so detained, to pay subsistence allowance :

Provided, also, that he shall not be released from such detention under clause (ii) or clause (iii), without the order of the Court.

[5][(1A) For the removal of doubts, it is hereby declared that no order for detention of the judgment-debtor in civil prison in execution of a decree for the payment of money shall be made, where the total amount of the decree does not exceed [6][two thousand rupees.]]

(2) A judgment-debtor released from detention under this section shall not merely by reason of his release be discharged from his debt, but he shall not be liable to be re-arrested under the decree in execution of which he was detained in the civil prison.

CHAPTER 10
Conclusion

There are numerous areas of daily life where quasi-judicial decisions affect the lives of ordinary people. Our constitution envisages a welfare state in which every citizen must have justice – social, economical and political. During performance of its functions, the State has to strike a balance between the competing private rights of the citizens and the interests of the State. The increased role of government in a welfare state has brought about a proliferation of disputes between the citizens and the government departments. Again, the subjects of dispute are so complex and technical that the conventional judges can hardly cope up with. The number of such disputes is also too big to be handled by the traditional court system. These disputes can often be better dealt with by experts in the respective fields rather than by conventional judges. It is not an exaggeration to say that the administrative adjudicators render more decisions than the judges decide in the traditional court system. Thus the administrative justice is increasingly considered not only on the basis of rule of law, but as a necessity of good governance.

Nevertheless, there are some of the disadvantages of the system of administrative justice. One of the serious problems facing the system is 'departmental bias'. It connotes the predilection of the inquiry officer towards the department/policy to which he is committed administratively. For instance, a Provident Fund Commissioner is committed to bring more number of factories under the fold of the Provident Fund Act and to extend the social security benefits to the workers employed in those factories. When an employer of a factory challenges the applicability of the provisions of the Provident Fund Act to his factory, the Commissioner happens to occupy the quasi-judicial chair as an adjudicator of the dispute. Having a duty to bring more number of factories under the PF Act's fold, he cannot be entirely indifferent to the issue before him. Often, they evade passing of orders against the interest of the department they belong to, even if evidences are remarkably in favour of the defendant/employer. More often than not they consider it 'anti-departmental' to pass such order, even if the preponderance of evidences warrant them not to do so. Such tendency on the part of the officers occupying quasi-judicial chairs, if not checked effectively, may negate the very concept of fairness in the administrative proceedings.

Lord Denning said, '*Justice must be rooted in confidence: and confidence is destroyed when right-minded people go away thinking "the judge was biased"*.' Those who sit on the quasi-judicial chair should act conscientiously to avoid bias of any kind, especially official bias and preserve public trust and confidence in the system of administrative adjudication.

APPENDIX

IMPORTANT AND USEFUL JUDICIAL PRONOUNCEMENTS RELATING TO QUASI-JUDICIAL PROCEEDINGS

- The basic test, therefore, for distinguishing between an administrative decision and a quasi-judicial decision is whether the decision of the statutory authority is based solely and exclusively on the application of legal principles or objective standards to the facts found on the material placed before it without any extraneous considerations or it is guided by considerations of policy or expediency and is based on the subjective satisfaction of the statutory authority. [*Sandhi Mamad Kala vs State Of Gujarat*[110]]

- Legal action cannot be initiated on the basis of a notice, which was sent by Registered Post, but returned by the Department of Post with the remark 'Not Found.'[*Union of India vs. Dinanath Shantaram*[111]]

- Where service of notice is not proved, employer's contention of non-providing the opportunity of hearing cannot be rejected. [*Gosalia Shipping (P) Ltd., vs. RPFC*[112]]

- Proceedings under Section 7A being quasi-judicial are governed by the principles of natural justice, meaning that the employer is given sufficient opportunity to represent his case fully, to see the report of the Inspector and other documents on record, and to put up his own evidences, if any. [*Gunvantri Harivallabh Jani vs. RPFC*[113]]

---

[110] (1973) 14 GLR 384
[111] , 1998 LLR 1097
[112] 1997(75)FLR609, 1997 Lab.I.C.3256
[113] 1970 AIR MP221, 1970 Lab IC 1383 MP High Court

- Grant of reasonable opportunity includes divulgence of the materials concerned which goes against the employer and to offer his opportunity to defend his case/offer his explanation. [*C.Dhanvantrai & Co. vs. Mahesh Kumar*[114],]

- Natural justice requires that copy of the Inspector's report on which the Department relies its case, must be supplied to the employer.[*RPFC vs. Glamour*[115]]

- Workers of the establishment are entitled to participate in an inquiry under Section 7A as interveners [*Mandavi Pellets Ltd. vs. RPFC*[116]]

- It is the legal duty of the Provident Fund Commissioners to exercise his powers to collect evidence and collate all material, before coming to proper conclusion – especially when a party to the proceedings requests for summoning evidence from a particular person. [*Food Corporation of India vs. RPFC*[117],]

- In deciding a matter quasi-judicially, the decision of the authority is not to be influenced by the departmental instructions – rather he is to go by his own best judgment [*Rajagopala Naidi vs.State Transport Appellate Tribunal*[118]].

- An inquiry under Section 7A is not an investigation under Section 2(h) of the Criminal Procedure Code, 1973. [*Provident Fund Inspector vs. Mohammed*[119],]

- The principle that emerges from the decisions referred to above is that an adjudicating authority which exercises quasi-judicial powers and discharges quasi-judicial functions cannot in the absence of any specific conferment of power, challenge an order passed by the Appellate

---

[114] 1994 (69) FLR 584 Bombay HC
[115] 1982 Lab I.C 1787 Delhi HC
[116] 1994, Lab I.C 1989, 1994(68) FLR 1134, Bombay HC
[117] 1990(60) FLR 15, 1990 SCC (L & S)1
[118] AIR 1964 SC 1573
[119] 1980 Ker LT 698 (DB)

Authority. [*Assistant Provident Fund Commissioner vs. West Coast Petroleum Agency[120]*]

- The authorities competent to make determination of dues under Section 7A of the Employees' Provident Funds and Miscellaneous Provisions Act 1952 are not authorized to delegate their powers.[*Ganesh Das Kaluram* vs. *Regional P.F.Commissioner[121],*]

- In *Union of India vs. A.N.Saxena*, it was contended that no disciplinary proceedings could be initiated against the respondent – Income Tax Officer regarding his judicial or quasi-judicial functions in making the assessment orders in question. The Supreme Court rejecting that contention held: 'In our view, an argument that no disciplinary action can be taken in regard to actions taken or purposed to be done in the course of judicial or quasi-judicial proceedings is not correct. It is true that when an officer is performing judicial or quasi-judicial functions, disciplinary proceedings regarding any of his actions in the course of such proceedings should be taken only after great caution and a close scrutiny of his actions and only if the circumstances so warrant. The initiation of such proceedings, it is true, is likely to shake the confidence of the public in the officer concerned and also if lightly taken to undermine his independence…Where the actions of such an officer indicate culpability, namely, a desire to oblige himself or unduly favour one of the parties or an improper motive there is no reason why disciplinary action should not be taken.'

CRIMINAL PROCEEDINGS AND DEPARTMENAL INQUIRY CAN GO SIMULTANEOUSLY

Departmental proceedings and criminal case are separate and distinct and can go on simultaneously. The object and purpose of departmental proceedings is to determine whether the delinquent officer is guilty of misconduct. Disciplinary proceedings are

---

[120] W.P(C) No.32393 of 2011, Kerala HC
[121] (1973) 2 LLJ 465 (Ori.)

initiated for the purpose of maintaining discipline and efficiency in public service. Criminal prosecution is launched for an offence of breach of law, which implies infringement of public duty punishable under criminal law as distinguished from mere private rights in disciplinary proceedings[*Hindustan Petroleum Corporation Ltd vs. Sarvesh Berry*[122]].

This aspect has been examined by the Apex Court in Depot Manager, APSRTC vs. Mohd. Yousuf Miya (1997) 2 SCC 699: State of Rajasthan vs. B.K.Meena (1996) 6 SCC 417 and other cases. In the case of State of Rajasthan vs. B.K.Meena (supra) after referring to several judgments, the Apex Court concluded:

(i) Departmental proceedings and proceedings in a criminal case can proceed simultaneously as there is no bar in their being conducted simultaneously, though separately.

(ii) If the departmental proceedings and the criminal case are based on identical and similar set of facts and the charge in the criminal case against the delinquent employee is of a grave nature, which involves complicated question of law and fact, it would be desirable to stay the departmental proceedings till the conclusion of the criminal case.

(iii) Whether the nature of a charge in a criminal case is grave and whether complicated question of fact and law are involved in that case, will depend upon the nature of offence, the nature of case launched against the employee on the basis of evidence and material collected against him during investigation or as reflected in the charge-sheet.

(iv) The factors mentioned at (ii) and (iii) above cannot be considered in isolation to stay the departmental proceedings but due regard has to be given to the fact that the departmental proceedings cannot be unduly delayed.

(v) If the criminal case does not proceed or its disposal is being unduly delayed, the departmental proceedings, even

---

[122] (2005)10SCC 471

if they were stayed on account of the pendency of the criminal case, can be resumed and proceeded with so as to conclude them at an early date, so that if the employee is found not guilty his honour may be vindicated and in case he is found guilty, the administration may get rid of him at the earliest. (*Brahma Prakash Kalra vs.National Thermal Power Corporation and Ors*, 2008)

RESIGNATION PENDING INQUIRY

By entering into contract of employment, a person does not sign a bond of slavery and a permanent employee cannot be deprived of his right to resign. A resignation by an employee would however normally require to be accepted by the employer, in order to be effective. It can be read in certain circumstances an employer would be justified in refusing to accept an employee's resignation as for instance when an employee wants to leave in the middle of a work in which his presence and participation are necessary.

An employer can also refuse to accept resignation when there is a disciplinary enquiry pending against an employee. If he is allowed to resign when an enquiry is pending against him, it would enable him to escape the consequences of adverse findings against him. Therefore on such occasion the employer is justified in not accepting the resignation [*Central Inland Water Transport Corporation Ltd vs. Tarunkanti Sengupta and another*[123]]

- There can be no estoppels against a statute

- It is a settled position in law that there cannot be *estoppel* against a statute. The Government cannot claim immunity based on the doctrine of *promissory estoppel*[124].

- Issues not raised before the Quasi-Judicial bodies can be raised before High Court through Writ under certain Circumstances

---

[123] 1986 II LLJ 171 SC

[124] The doctrine of promissory *estoppel* prevents one party from withdrawing a promise made to a second party if the latter has reasonably relied on that promise

- *In Rattan Lal Sharma vs. Managing Committee, Dr Hari Ram (Co- education) Higher Secondary School* : [125] the Supreme Court held : 'But if the plea though not specifically raised before the subordinate tribunals or the administrative and quasi-judicial bodies, is raised before the High Court in the writ proceeding for the first time and the plea goes to the root of the question and is based on admitted and uncontroverted facts and does not require any further investigation into a question of fact, the High Court is not only justified in entertaining the plea but in the anxiety to do justice which is the paramount consideration of the court, it is only desirable that a litigant should not be shut out from raising such plea which goes to the root of the *lis* involved.

- **Demarcation line between Administrative Order and a Quasi-judicial order is getting thinned**

  The Supreme Court in the case of *Rajesh Kumar & Other vs Dy CIT and Others*[126] observed, 'in any event, when civil consequences ensue, there is hardly any distinction between an administrative order and a quasi-judicial order. There might have been difference of opinions at one point of time, but it is now well-settled that a thin demarcated line between an administrative order and quasi-judicial order now stands obliterated.'

- 'The order of a judicial or quasi-judicial authority is not final for the purpose of *resjudicata* during the time allowed for filing an appeal or the pendency of an appeal. In the absence of any statutory provision to the contrary, or an interim stay granted by a competent authority, the order, although not final, is provisionally executable, subject to restoration [K.P. Abdul Kareem Hajee v. ITO].

- **Need for an Speaking Order**

---

[125] (1993) 4 SCC 10
[126] (2007) 2 SCC 181

The recording of reasons which lead to the passing of the order is basically intended to serve a two-fold purpose:

(i) that the 'party aggrieved' acquires knowledge of the reasons and, in a proceeding before the High Court or the Supreme Court (since there is no right of appeal or revision), it has an opportunity to demonstrate that the reasons which persuaded the authority to pass an order adverse to his interest were erroneous, irrational or irrelevant, and(2) that the obligation to record reasons and convey the same to the party concerned operates as a deterrent against possible arbitrary action by the quasi-judicial or the executive authority invested with judicial powers.[Bidhannagar (Salt Lake) Welfare vs. Central Valuation Board]127

- **Wrong mention/Non-mentioning of law**

  Wrong mention or non-mentioning of a provision of law would not invalidate a valid order which is otherwise valid one. [*Allauddin Charities And Zakath vs Hameed Ali And Ors.*][128]

- **Application of the Limitation Act of 1963**

  The Limitation Act, 1963 is applicable only in relation to certain applications and not all applications despite the fact that the words 'other proceedings' were added in the long title of the Act in 1963. The provisions of the said Act are not applicable to the proceedings before bodies other than courts, such as quasi-judicial tribunal or even an executive authority. The Act primarily applies to the civil proceedings or some special criminal proceedings. Even in a Tribunal, where the Code of Civil Procedure or Code of Criminal Procedure is applicable; the Limitation Act, 1963 per se may not be applied to the proceedings

---

127 Appeal (civil) 5519-5520 of 2007

128 2002 (1) ALD 67, 2002 (2) ALT 534

before it. Even in relation to certain civil proceedings, the Limitation Act may not have any application. As for example, there is no bar of limitation for initiation of a final decree proceedings or to invoke the jurisdiction of the Court under Section 151 of the Code of Civil Procedure or for correction of accidental slip or omission in judgments, orders or decrees; the reason being that these powers can be exercised even *suo motu* by the Court and, thus, no question of any limitation arises. [See Nityananda, M. Joshi and another vs. the Life Insurance Corporation of India and others, AIR 1970 SC 209, Hindustan Times Ltd. vs. Union of India and Others, (1998) 2 SCC 242 and Mt. Laxmibai (supra)]Even no period of limitation is prescribed in relation to a writ proceeding.[**L.S. Synthetics Ltd vs Fairgrowth Financial Services**][129]

- **Which is a 'quasi-judicial' body?**

In *Brijnandan Sinha v. Jyoti Narain*[130], it has been held that any Tribunal or authority whose decision is final and binding between the parties is a court. In the said decision, the Supreme Court, while deciding a case under the Court of Enquiry Act held that a court of enquiry is not a court as its decision is neither final nor binding upon the parties. In *Virindar Kumar Satyawadi v. State of Punjab*[131], the Supreme Court has made a broad distinction of a court and quasi judicial Tribunal. In the *Sitamarhi Central Cooperative Bank Ltd. v. Jugal Kishore Sinha*[132], a Division Bench of this Court has held Assistant Registrars appointed under the Bihar and Orissa Co-operative Societies Act to be courts. In the said decision, this Court has held that, when a question arises as to whether the authority constituted under a particular Act exercising judicial or quasi-judicial power is a court or not, then the

---

[129] Appeal (civil) 4268 of 2003
[130] AIR 1956 SC 66,
[131] AIR 1956 SC 153
[132] AIR 1965 Pat 227

following tests must be fulfilled before the said authority can be termed as a court : --

(a) the dispute .which is to be decided by him must be in the nature of a civil suit;

(b) the procedure for determination of such dispute must be judicial procedure; and

(c) the decision must be of a binding nature.

- **Quasi-Judicial bodies to follow the legislative intent**

Power delegated by statute is limited by its terms and subordinate to its objects. The delegate must act in good faith, reasonably intra vires the power granted, and on relevant consideration of material facts. All his decisions whether characterized as legislative or administrative or quasi-judicial must be in harmony with the constitution and other laws of the land. They must be 'reasonably related to the purposes of enabling legislation' See Leila Mourning v. Family Publications Service (1973) 411 US 356, 36 Law Ed. 2d 318. If they are manifestly unjust or oppressive or outrageous or directed to an unauthorized end or do not tend in some degree to the accomplishment of the objects of delegation, Courts might well say,' Parliment never intended to give authority to make such rules; they are unreasonable and ultra vires.'[*M/s. Shri Sitaram Sugar Co. Ltd. v. Union of India*][133]

---

[133] AIR 1990 SC 1277

LIST OF IMPORTANT LEGAL TERMS

Sl.	Legal Term	Meaning
1	Affidavit	A statement, which before being signed, the person signing takes an oath that, the contents are, to the best of their knowledge, true. It is also signed by a notary or some other judicial officer that can administer oaths, to the effect that the person signing the affidavit was under oath when doing so. These documents carry great weight in Courts to the extent that judges frequently accept an affidavit instead of the testimony of the witness.
2	Alternative dispute resolution (ADR)	A procedure for settling a dispute outside the courtroom. Most forms of ADR are not binding, and involve referral of the case to a neutral party such as an arbitrator or mediator.
3	Burden of proof	The duty to prove disputed facts. In civil cases, a plaintiff generally has the burden of proving his or her case. In criminal cases, the prosecution has the burden of proving the defendant's guilt.
4	*De facto*	Latin, meaning 'in fact' or 'actually.' Something that exists in fact but not as a matter of law.
5	*De jure*	Latin, meaning 'in law.' Something that exists by operation of law.
6	*De novo*	Latin, meaning 'anew.' A trial de novo is a completely new trial. Appellate review de novo implies no deference to the trial judge's ruling.
7	Docket	A log containing the complete history of each case in the form of brief chronological entries summarizing the court proceedings.
8	*Ex parte*	A proceeding brought before a court by one party only, without notice to or challenge by the other side.
9	*In forma pauperis*	'In the manner of a pauper.' Permission given by the court to a person to file a case without

		payment of the required court fees because the person cannot pay them.
10	*Pro se*	Representing oneself. Serving as one's own lawyer.
11	*Bona fide*	In good faith
12	*Carte Blanche*	A signature of a person on a piece of paper having blank spaces to write anything on it
13	Caveat	A formal notice given by a party interested in the proceeding (This literally means '*let him beware*')
14	Cognizable offence	An offence for which the suspected person can be arrested without a warrant
15	*Contra jus*	Against the law
16	*Contra legem*	Against the law of the land
17	Dispose	Act of terminating a judicial proceeding
18	Estop	To stop, bar or impede
19	Estoppel	a rule of law which prevents a person from alleging or denying a fact, because of his/her own previous act
20	*et al*	an abbreviation of et alia meaning 'and others'
21	*et ano*	And another.
22	Ex parte	a proceeding, order, motion, application, request, submission etc., made by or granted for the benefit of one party only; done for, in behalf of, or on application of one party only
23	expunge	the authorized act of physically destroying information, in files, computers or other depositories
24	fair preponderance	Level of proof in a civil action; more than half; more convincing.
25	garnish	to attach a portion of the wages or other property of a debtor to secure repayment of the debt
26	garnishee	A person who owes a debt to a judgment debtor, or a person other than the judgment debtor who has property in his/her possession or custody in which a judgment debtor has an interest
27	Alias Summons	A second or subsequent summons issued after

		the originally issued summons expires without being served.
28	*Delegatus non potest Delegare*	A delegate cannot delegate. In other words, a person to whom an authority or decision-making power has been delegated to from a higher source, cannot, in turn, delegate again to another, unless the original delegation explicitly authorized it.
29	*Donatio Mortis Causa*	A deathbed gift, made by a dying person, with the intent that the person receiving the gift shall keep the thing if death ensues. Such a gift is exempted from the estate of the deceased as property is automatically conveyed upon death. In most jurisdictions, real property cannot be transferred by these deathbed gifts.
	Exonerate	To free from suspicion; to show someone to be free of guilt.
30	*Inter alia*	Latin: 'among other things', 'for example' or 'including'.
31	Interlocutory	Proceedings taken during the course of, and incidental to a trial.
32	*mens rea*	Latin for 'guilty mind.' Many serious crimes require the proof of '*mens rea*' before a person can be convicted. In other words, the prosecution must prove not only that the accused committed the offence but also that he (or she) did it knowing that it was prohibited; that their act (or omission) was done with an intent to commit a crime.
33	*Nemo judex in parte sua*	Latin and a fundamental principle of natural justice, which states that no person can judge a case in which he or she is party. May also be called *nemo judex in sua causa* or *nemo debet esse judex in propria causa*.
34	Onus	Latin for 'The burden'. It is usually used in the context of evidence. The onus of proof in criminal cases lies with the state. It is the state that has the burden of proving beyond reasonable doubt. In civil cases, the onus of

		proof lies with the plaintiff who must prove his case by balance of probabilities. So 'onus' refers both to the party with the burden, and to the scope of that burden, the latter depending whether the context is criminal or civil.
35	*Pari delicto*	Latin for 'of equal fault.' For example, if two parties complain to a judge of the non-performance of a contract by the other, the judge could refuse to provide a remedy to either of them because of *'pari delicto'*: a finding that they were equally at fault in causing the contract's breach.
36	*Pari passu*	Latin: Equitably and without preference. This term is often used in bankruptcy proceedings where creditors are said to be *'pari passu'* which means that they are all equal and that distribution of the assets will occur without preference between them.
37	*Prima facie*	The term *'prima facie case'* refers to those facts that will establish a party's right to legal relief if no evidence to the contrary is offered by the party's opponent. The term 'prima facie evidence' refers to evidence that is sufficient to prove a fact unless overcome by other evidence.
38	*Res judicata*	Latin: A matter that has already been conclusively decided by a court and cannot be re-litigated.
39	*Stare decisis*	The doctrine that the decisions of the court should serve as precedents for future cases.
40	*Sub judice*	A matter that is still under consideration by a court.
41	*Subpoena*	Latin: an order of a court that requires a person to be present at a certain time and place or suffer a penalty (subpoena means, literally, 'under penalty')
42	Testimony	The statement of a witness under oath that is given as evidence.
43	Verbatim	The recording of the exact word-for-word

		proceedings of a trial court, as prepared in transcript format.
44	Void *ab initio*	Legally not binding
45	Doctrine of Eclipse	This doctrine is applicable to pre-Constitutional laws only. It implies that an existing law which violates fundamental right is not dead or void per-se but only becomes unenforceable. 'It is over shadowed or eclipsed by the fundamental rights and remains dormant but it is not dead.'
46	*Sine die*	Adjournment sine die means 'without assigning a day for further hearing'
47	*Lis alibi pendens*	dispute elsewhere pending

BIBLIOGRAPHY

Andhra Pradesh Vigilance Manual. (n.d.). Retrieved April 29, 2012, from Andhra Pradesh Vigilance Commission: http://apvc.ap.nic.in/js/vol1/c22t1s5.html

Bilal, N. M. (2004). *Dynamism of Judicial Control and Administrative Adjudication.* Deep and Deep Publications.

Brahma Prakash Kalra vs.National Thermal Power Corporation and Ors, IPA 223/2002 (Delhi High Court March 17, 2008).

G.J. Kanga And Anr. vs S.S. Basha on 18 August, 1992 (Bombay High Court August 18, 1982).

H.M.Seervai. (1984). *Constitutional Law of India: A cirtical commentary* volume 2.

Hunter, S. L. (2009). *You be the Judge.*

Jackson, O. P. (2001). *Constitutional and Administrative Law* (8 ed.). London: Sweet & Maxwell.

Murthy, P. (2006). *Consumer Justice.* New Delhi: Indian Institute of Public Administration.